Climbing Roses

BY

HELEN VAN PELT WILSON

DRAWINGS BY

LÉONIE BELL

M. BARROWS AND COMPANY, INC. *New York* 1955

For my cherished friend
Alice Bond Newnham

Contents

Thanks to You

THE COMPLETION of a book always finds me in tremendous debt to many people—for *patience* with me first of all, since the engrossed writer is not always the easiest of companions or associates; for *assistance,* since the knowledge and experience of many horticulturists must be reflected in a book dealing with any special area, as here that of the Climbing Rose. I am therefore most grateful to:

Léonie Bell, a fellow fragrance-enthusiast, who has done the drawings for this book (as she did for both my books on African Violets), and whose thoughtful criticism and garden notes have contributed so very much to the text as well. Besides being a gifted artist, Mrs. Bell is a professional horticulturist, a graduate of the School of Horticulture for Women at Ambler, Pennsylvania. Although she is the devoted mother of four small children, she has not been deterred from sharing with me this wonderful adventure of writing a book about the roses we both admire.

Richard Thomson who has cooperated with Mrs. Bell in permitting her to draw specimens in his garden in Wynnewood, Pennsylvania; and with me in reading and most helpfully criticizing the complete manuscript.

Charles H. Perkins, President of Jackson & Perkins, who on one of the busiest days of his always-busy year, with visitors and reporters hard upon him, gave me uninterrupted hours of discussion and a wonderful travelogue through his magnificent display gardens at Newark, New York.

Mr. and Mrs. Walter D. Brownell who have in days of thoughtful discussion at their home and in their gardens at Little Compton, Rhode Island, shared their deep knowledge of the roses of the present and their high hopes for those of the future.

W. Dexter Brownell, Jr., who facilitated my trips to Little Compton, answered my innumerable questions both by letter and in interviews, and made easier the always stiff ascent toward the completion of a manuscript; and to Mrs. Brownell, too, whose hospitality at their lovely place on the Sakonnet River was so much appreciated.

Will Tillotson, first for the pleasure of his catalog and the books on Old Roses which it brought to my happy attention, but also for the critical advice he found time to give me on the text, both by letter and during his recent visit to New York.

Ray C. Allen, author of *Roses for Every Garden,* who assisted me in the development of my new classification for climbers and has taught me—as well as thousands of others—so much about the culture of the rose.

Ruth W. Spears, my dear friend and author of many Barrows books, who through the years has shared garden pilgrimages with me and made for my recent guidance clever drawings of the many ways we saw the climbers supported. She has also permitted my use of some of the patterns for fences, etc. which are part of her Home Workshop Pattern Service.

Everett A. Piester, Director of Parks and Recreation, at Hartford, Connecticut, who, on a hot rainy June day, gave Mrs. Spears and me a truly wonderfully conducted tour of the Memorial Rose Garden at Elizabeth Park; and to Mrs. Piester, also, who solaced us with luncheon.

Rosalie F. Doolittle, who advised me on the proper selection of climbers for the Southwest.

Margaret and Harry O'Brien and the Columbus rosarians, who gave me a never-to-be-forgotten dinner party and then generously shared with me their wealth of rose experiences.

B. B. Coyne of Seattle and *Helene and Nat Schoen* of Vancouver, Washington; the *A. H. Neicks* of San Francisco; the *van Barnevelds, John Senior and John Junior,* of Los Angeles, all of whom interrupted busy schedules to make it possible for me, on my recent trip to the West, to see local rose gardens and to develop sound regional lists of climbers.

Larry Hilaire of Portland, Oregon for a wonderful "rose dinner" at his Encore Restaurant.

James P. Gurney, Secretary of The American Rose Society, whose service to members is phenomenally prompt and whose answers to my many questions were always helpful. I am particularly grateful for his guidance, advice, and hospitality on the occasion of my visit to Columbus and my tour of the wonderful new Columbus Park of Roses.

The American Rose Society for sponsoring, with J. Horace McFarland Company, that invaluable compilation of roses and their sources, *Modern Roses IV.*

Roy E. Shepherd for writing such an excellent book as *History of the Rose.* I am sure all future students of this flower will share my gratitude.

Catherine E. Meickle for her excellent analysis of rose fragrance in her article in *Horticulture* in June, 1953.

Enid Grote, Librarian of The Horticulture Society of New York, without whom I could never expect to manage any project of research involving horticulture.

New York   HELEN VAN PELT WILSON
September, 1954

CLIMBING ROSES

CHAPTER ONE

Loveliest of Plants

How LOVELY ARE the Climbing Roses which bring to the "leafy month of June" glowing color, matchless grace, and often a sweet heady fragrance. What possibilities of beauty lie in just a single well-grown plant which, commencing in early summer, may, before autumn frost, produce literally thousands of blossoms. Even the "once-bloomers" like Silver Moon, bear a tremendous burden of beauty when they grow loftily covering the side of a house, while the recurrent flowering of Blaze, New Dawn, Pink Cloud, and the Everblooming Brownell Pillars is a repeated miracle of lavish color from early summer into fall.

In all my gardens there have been Climbing Roses, sometimes as frameworks of beauty, backgrounds for other plants like shrubs or perennials, sometimes as twining companions for clematis. Yet a garden in the strict sense is not their necessary setting. If you have a house with four walls, four climbers will have room; yes, even on the cold side, unless the climate is really severe. Long ago Climbing Lady Ashtown graced my north breakfast-room casement in southern New Jersey, and grew so tall there I could pick the exquisite pointed pink-and-yellow buds from the bedroom window above. On the south wall of the same house, Silver Moon and Gardenia beautifully covered one gabled end clear to the third floor. I never made visits during their matchless weeks of silver-and-gold enchantment; indeed, I never willingly left my house in June.

Today at Stony Brook Cottage, Golden Climber is a special joy. Covering the front half of my white clapboard house, it sends forth long energetic canes to adorn the peaked roof of the entrance. And it embroiders the window sill of the guest room with long-stemmed, shapely yellow buds which come at regular intervals along a cane, trained parallel to the window. When the great, golden, fragrant flowers open, their beauty is repeated within by a wallpaper which also flaunts a pattern of exuberant yellow roses.

On the Small Place

On the small property, the suburban lot, for instance, Climbing Roses have a most proper place. Let them adorn the entrance of the house or cover the essential barrier at the line where "good fences make good neighbors." Or train them perhaps over treillage built to shield a little service area; or, where the ground is full of boulders, give up thoughts of lawn and plant Trailing Roses which have artistic affinity for rocks of all colors and conditions.

Where a homesite has the old-time "stone fences," as here in New England, Climbing Roses have a wonderful opportunity, especially such rampant varieties as Mary Wallace, on whom I have bestowed a whole boundary. Elsewhere over an extensive post-and-rail fence and also on a long snow fence, which, cut in half, wanders irregularly to separate lawn from black-eyed Susans and Queen Anne's lace of meadow, grow such Trailing Roses as Carpet of Gold.

1. A garden arch neatly adorned with a Climbing Rose. *(Mary Deputy Lamson, L. A.; Richard Averill Smith, Photo)*

2. Behold, "the triumphant Climbing Rose, the exhausted, tottering support!" (*Roche, Photo*)

3. A brilliant Climbing Rose in the garden of the Mission San Miguel in Arcangel, California. *(Josef Muench, Photo)*

4. Exuberant bloom on a Climbing Rose at the seashore.
(*McFarland, Photo*)

5. Climbing Roses and rocks in a New England setting beside a lake. *(Gottscho-Schleisner, Photo)*

6. New Dawn grown as a Shrub in the corner of a garden wall. (*McFarland, Photo*)

7. Elegance in an alabaster vase with Climbing Hybrid Teas and clematis. *(Myra Brooks, Arrangement; Roche, Photo)*

8. Yellow Climbing Roses with brown driftwood and green fennel. (*Margaret Carrick, Arrangement and Photo*)

Carpet of Gold is a plant no one should do without. And no one does who once sees mine in fullness of bloom.

In the Garden

And in a garden, small or large, what opportunities there are to enjoy the climbers. On arches and pillars (though I care least for these), over pergola or summer house or long covered walk—everywhere they are delightful. But of where to plant climbers, I shall have more to say anon.

Assets Galore

Now I would bring briefly to your attention the simplicity of their culture. If you have never grown a rose, start with the climbers. If you have grown only the Hybrid Teas, and they have worn you down, their demands going beyond your capacity for labors of love in the garden, by all means plant the climbers. They are less demanding as to soil, will produce satisfactorily with little or no feeding and spraying, are in many instances of below-zero hardiness, and of an almost everlasting constitution. Many a Climbing Rose has outlived the hands that planted it.

I think, for instance, of four neglected climbers, which I see flowering at a nearby farm. The Paul's Scarlet covers the side and roof of a low outbuilding. Gardenia, American Pillar, and Dr. W. Van Fleet, I think it is, ramble over the fence. All have been there, the family tells me, for decades. Others speak of generations-old climbers. What more can the casual gardener or the busy gardener, who is also concerned with lawn, trees, shrubs, perennials, and annuals, ask of a plant than is freely supplied by the well-chosen Climbing Rose?

The Right Climber for You

Wherever you live there are lovely climbers suited to your climate and situation. In some favored locations the beautiful possibilities are almost bewildering. In the South for instance, at Charleston, the violet-scented White Banksia, like its Chinese ancestor, climbs to 60 feet, blooming in late winter with the white lace of azaleas. In Florida and Georgia, where it has been named state flower, the Cherokee in May or June spreads a fragrant enchantment of large, fluffy-stamened, pure-white flowers on canes that trail or climb to 15 feet or more. Its beautiful daughter, Silver Moon, graces our northern gardens with equal beauty. And who can forget the scented loveliness of Climbing Teas in the Deep South—the creamy Perle des Jardins, the amber-flushed, pale-pink Gloire de Dijon? Or in California, the magnificence of the single, pale-yellow Mermaid with its sweet wild-rose fragrance?

If ever a Climbing Rose is a disappointment—and only grudgingly do I admit the possibility—it is usually because the right type has not been chosen for a particular purpose. Perhaps a tender variety has been planted where a hardy one was required, or strong fragrance or recurrent bloom was expected where no possibilities of these existed, since the best cultural practices cannot produce what Nature does not originally bestow.

I recall my exasperation in Philadelphia the second summer of New Dawn's enthusiastic residence with me when, week after week, I mounted a ladder in the heat to cut back rampant, energetic canes. Finally I admitted that conformity to my slight garden arch was an impossibility, even with constant supervision. As the summer waned—and I with it— the arch seemed to stagger under its beautiful burden rather than to be adorned by it. This is, of course, a common sight —the triumphant Climbing Rose, the exhausted, tottering support.

But what a wonder plant is this same New Dawn when permitted a field of conquest commensurate with its power. I think of its unbelievable pink beauty on the white façade of a home I visit in northern New Jersey. There it grows in a great 15-foot sweep to the second-floor bedrooms, and is held by strong cords to the turquoise-blue ironwork of a balcony. How enchanting it is to awaken there on a summer morning to New Dawn's delicate scent and to enjoy the seashell-perfect blossoms right at one's window.

The owner has these pleasures because she chose a rose of proper qualities for her purpose and taste; in this case, sufficient height, large blooms of a pink that particularly pleased her, glossy disease-resistant foliage to leave her almost untroubled, and a reliable, recurrent habit of bloom as well.

For you, too, there are just-right Climbing Roses; in red undoubtedly if you are a man, in yellow or pink probably for feminine pleasure (though I myself love white roses). You can have trailers and climbers from 5 to 40 feet; colors, pure and clear, or of indescribably beautiful blendings; the tiny blooms of Minnehaha or the enormous blossoms of Peace; the wild-rose simplicity of Evangeline or the elegant sophistication of King Midas; old-rose or damask perfume or the fragrance of tea or blends of these; power to endure way-below-zero cold and to withstand or ignore onslaughts of pest and disease.

Which Climbing Roses will you have? Let us examine all the many fascinating possibilities, so that when *you* choose, it will be wisely.

But not all the qualities you desire or admire may be present in one Climbing Rose. Perhaps we do not yet have the perfect variety, but surely it is very near, as many recent introductions proclaim. So, before you select, know the qualities most important to you, but first, what *is* a Climbing Rose?

CHAPTER TWO

The Roses that "Climb"

HEIRS OF THE AGES, natives of the world's far-flung waste-lands, swamps, and fertile meadows, Climbing Roses are a complex group and their modern counterparts rich with diverse strains. Actually the "Climbing" Rose is not a rose that climbs—at least not in the botanical sense. Rose plants do not produce the tiny suction disks of Virginia creeper, the petioles of clematis, or the tendrils of grape. They do not twine in the manner of honeysuckle or hop, or bear the aerial roots of English ivy. Generally speaking, the Climbing Rose is just a tall-growing plant which must be trained and tied, if it is to grace attractively an arch, fence, trellis or pergola.

Occasionally of its own volition it will clamber up a tree, especially in the wild. It is reported that the species, *Rosa Banksiae,* in southern China grows to the top of forest giants, and I have seen Climbing Summer Snow in a New York garden fling itself from a tall arch to an adjacent red pine and travel up 5 feet more to 15 feet or so. At a seashore garden in Cape May County in New Jersey, Excelsa mounts the tall shining holly trees, while on neglected properties everywhere, various old climbers, unaided, travel vigorously up and around, if a tree stands conveniently at hand.

Even the division between climber and bush rose is arbitrary. Many a Hybrid Perpetual or Rugosa can be as well trained to trellis or fence as a true "climber." The Moss Rose, Jeanne de Montfort, and the Shrub Rose, Fragrant Beauty, will easily cover a 6- to 7-foot pillar. Of course, none of these will travel the vast distances of a City of York or Dr. Huey; still many of the old-fashioned bush roses can be induced to "climb" far enough to drape a wall with color and so inform the passing breeze with scent. And who astounded by the "Shrub" Rose, Skyrocket, flowering on a pillar, would call it a "bush" rose?

Perhaps we should go back to William Paul's century-old definition of Climbing Roses as "the most vigorous selected from various groups." Conveniently this would include all species and varieties that require supports or are *adaptable* to growing on them. Many so-called climbers, we know, are equally lovely grown as shrubs, or even as ground-covers. I recall in Mr. Edwin De T. Bechtel's gardens in Bedford Village, New York, a 9-foot fountain of pink Dr. W. Van Fleet silhouetted against a high gray wall. It was handsome, indeed. True there were pole supporters placed far out at the sides to hold up the 12-foot spread of heavy blossom-laden branches, but here was Van Fleet as shrub not climber. And Dorothy Perkins in this part of the country is as content to travel over a field as to cover a doorway arch, and does both with a charming grace.

The Perfect Climbing Roses

Certainly today's glorious climbers have a rich and multiple heritage. Hybridizers have cunningly utilized the qualities of many species, and also those of hybrids, to produce them. Working in many parts of the world, but especially in England, Ireland, France, and Spain, as well as in the United States, they have combined available traits with varying emphasis, perhaps, as at the Brownells', growing 20,000 hybridized seedlings from which they may select but one promising variety to introduce. Selecting from both species and hybrids, all have sought to give us the *perfect* Climbing Rose. And that, both rosarians and average gardeners would agree, is a tall-growing plant, winter-hardy in root and branch, disease- and pest-free, everblooming in clear reds, pinks, yellows, white, and blends, and—fragrant.

In the main, they have worked from six primary sources: *Rosa multiflora* and *R. Wichuraiana* have made the greatest contributions to the climbers, but certainly not the only ones. From *R. setigera, R. arvensis, R. moschata,* and *R. sempervirens* have also come valuable elements; and, in lesser degree, *R. chinensis, R. odorata, R. borbonica, R. Banksiae, R. bracteata, R. laevigata, R. gallica, R. centifolia,* and *R. damascena* have released qualities of beauty, vigor, and fragrance.

A Valuable Ancestor (Rosa multiflora)

No more beautiful than a blossoming blackberry, which has after all a certain modest charm, the Japanese Rose, *Rosa multiflora,* produces in May and June pyramidal clusters of small, single, white flowers of sweet, honeylike fragrance on 12-foot arching canes. Naturally vigorous and adaptable to many situations, of moderate hardiness, unfortunately only once-blooming and very susceptible to mildew, it was the parent of the early Multiflora Ramblers. Extreme floriferousness and height are its major contributions, and also qualities that have to date made it unsurpassed as understock. The majority of Climbing Roses today are budded on this sturdy *R. multiflora,* which is economical to grow, no transmitter of blackspot, adaptable to many soils and climates (except in the extreme north and far south), not given to suckering, and capable of being budded over a long period. Furthermore, it is compatible with many rose types.

If you know the plant sold for a "living fence," you know multiflora. Graphically described as "horse high, bull strong, and goat tight," it has been the friend of many a farmer who required certain boundaries or had to deal with soil erosion. However, unless your property is extensive and plants with a 10- to 12-foot spread are acceptable, multiflora has no place —except as understock.

Receptive to the pollen of other roses, multiflora has produced important progeny. There are two forms of it which are well worth growing: the rather tender Seven Sisters or Grevillia Rose of 1815 *(Rosa multiflora platyphylla),* which bears variable, pink-to-crimson clusters, and the true-pink cathayensis, introduced in 1907, and a lovely thing. Both are from China. Crimson Rambler (introduced in 1893) and its improved form, Chevy Chase; the white Neige d'Avril (with the other most important climber as parent, *R. Wichuraiana);* pink Roserie; rose-to-white Tausendschön; Veilchenblau, and its improved form, Violette, with purple semidouble flowers, are still fairly familiar, especially in old gardens.

Important Progenitor (Rosa Wichuraiana)

Oddly enough Dorothy Perkins, which in 1901 really put Ramblers on the map, is not a close relative of Crimson Rambler, with which it is always compared, but a descendant of *Rosa Wichuraiana,* the Memorial Rose, also from Japan. This species, from which many of the fine new climbers have been bred, is itself so lovely that if you wish a Trailing Rose you need look no farther. The fragrant, white, few-flowered clusters appear abundantly through July, and the attractive foliage is glossy and more or less evergreen, depending on location. To veil a bank or border a flight of steps, this East Asian species is superb.

For breeding purposes, the later flowering of Wichuraiana with its midsummer tendency is an advantage, also its vigor and notable disease-resistance. The gleam of its foliage is usually apparent in most of its descendants, which include tall climbers like Silver Moon, pillar types like Breeze Hill, and Ramblers like the famous Dorothy Perkins, introduced by the Jackson & Perkins Company of Newark, New York, in 1901, still beloved in gardens the world over and a colorful wanderer in the fields, to which it has often escaped.

Wichuraiana has indeed been the hybridizer's delight from the time of the first exciting introductions of Michael H. Horvath's varieties, Pink Roamer and Evergreen Gem, by W. A. Manda of South Orange, New Jersey, in 1897 and 1899. Between 1901 and 1920, M. H. Walsh of Woods Hole, Massachusetts, introduced some forty varieties with clusters of various size, with single and double flowers, in colors from white to dark crimson. Perhaps the best of these are Evangeline, Excelsa, Hiawatha, Minnehaha, and Nokomis, not all available today except in old gardens or from collectors of Ramblers. Brownell's Everblooming Pillars, a group first presented in 1953, are magnificent modern hybrids of Wichuraiana ancestry.

It is also to the late Dr. Walter Van Fleet of Watsontown, Pennsylvania, that we are indebted for a tremendous number of handsome Wichuraiana climbers, all once-bloomers to be sure, although the everblooming New Dawn is a sport of his outstanding Dr. W. Van Fleet. Other long-time favorites developed by the Doctor are: Breeze Hill, Glenn Dale, Mary

Lovett, and Mary Wallace. The unsurpassed American Pillar was the result of his cross of *Rosa Wichuraiana, R. setigera,* and a red Hybrid Perpetual.

Van Fleet varieties have, indeed, stood the test of time. I notice whenever I visit a public rose garden as at Hartford, Connecticut, or private rose collections anywhere, that it is the old Van Fleet varieties which are so colorful and outstanding in June. I think you will discover too that as you assess any large planting from a distance, the Van Fleets always impress you on first glance.

A Native American Climber (Rosa setigera)

The Prairie or Michigan Rose, *Rosa setigera,* is our only native rose with a tendency to climb. Appearing in practically every state from the Atlantic Ocean to the Rocky Mountains, it flourishes in fields, pastures, and along roadways, particularly in the Midwest. Lovely in late June and July, when the slender recurving branches bear rosy 2-inch blossoms that soon fade to white, it is well worth your attention just as it is—unhybridized.

At Seven Mile Beach Island in New Jersey, Mr. George E. Lippincott grows setigera on two poles as sentinels at the entrance of his driveway. About 12 feet high, they produce single pink blooms that cover the plant and appear later than most other roses, and as such are particularly appreciated. Setigera has been sadly neglected for landscape effect, this eminent rosarian remarks.

By hybridizers, it has not been neglected. Horvath found it valuable, although he used it to play a minor role. Captain Kidd, Doubloons, Jean Lafitte, Long John Silver, Meda, Polaris (with *Rosa Wichuraiana* and *R. foetida bicolor*), Thor are all varieties of setigera parentage, and Dr. Van Fleet, as I have said, used it in American Pillar, which is probably setigera's most distinguished descendant. Various forms of the species, as Baltimore Belle, have also been employed as understock.

To the breeder of Climbing Roses, setigera offers vigorous 12- to 15-foot growth, disease-resistance, and obviously wide adaptability to soil and climate, but the latter within some limits. Plants show considerable winter injury in the most northern states. Setigera is, however, scentless, also difficult to bud, slow to root from cuttings, and seeds germinate very slowly, but that arching, lengthy habit and the midsummer bloom make it valuable, nonetheless.

Field Rose (Rosa arvensis)

In the Field Rose of Europe and especially of the British Isles, breeders of Climbing Roses found a species whose slender shoots grew 15 to 20 feet a season. Very early flowering and single, white, 2-inch blossoms of delicate fragrance were other assets. Here was a rose that could live and thrive under conditions of sun and shade likely to be intolerable for most other roses, and this was especially true of the Scottish Ayrshire Roses, of which *Rosa arvensis* is one parent. Canes to 30 feet in a season appear on the hybrid Ayrshires in their native land; in this country, they are less rampant. Few of the old varieties are available today, but Beacon Belle, Betty Alden, and Boston Beauty were introduced in 1919 by R. & J. Farquhar of Boston. Yet *R. arvensis* in the wild is lovely and, according to Roy E. Shepherd, this may well be the Musk Rose of Shakespeare and the White Rose of the House of York.

The Musk Rose (Rosa moschata)

The rose *commonly* called Musk is the ancient *Rosa moschata* from India or southern China. In warm, humid areas, it is tremendously vigorous and also tends to be remontant, both valuable qualities in hybridizing. Yet in this country the Musk Rose rarely exceeds 10 feet and blooms only occasionally after the July display; still its very lateness is valuable in a family that tends to heavy June flowering. The ivory-white flowers appear in clusters and have the so-called musk fragrance, faint by day, stronger at night.

The Hybrid Musks of the Reverend Joseph H. Pemberton of Essex, England, include the 8-foot Prosperity (1919) considered by some of us to be the handsomest double-white climber yet produced, and the fragrant, pink-budded white Kathleen (1922) which, reaching as high as 15 feet, is well suited to climbing or fence-growing. Francis E. Lester, an excellent American-produced Hybrid Musk, is of more recent origin, 1946; also Wind Chimes, a rose-pink, 15-foot beauty. (Of these, more in Chapter 7.)

The Noisettes (Rosa Noisettiana)

The Noisettes, supposedly crosses between *Rosa moschata* and *R. chinensis,* are the special glory of our southern gardens. The medium-sized, semidouble, blush-pink blossoms, sometimes 100 in a cluster, are borne at the ends of canes. Outstanding varieties have resulted from further crossings with the Tea Rose.

Noisettes are remontant, and some will even survive when grown in the North. Three relatively hardy ones—at least in Philadelphia—are Mme. Alfred Carrière, William Allen Richardson, and, if grown in very rich soil, Gloire de Dijon.

The latter is also classed as a Climbing Tea. In the South at least four more are of outstanding beauty, all fragrant, of course—Lamarque, Maréchal Niel, Rêve d'Or, and Solfaterre. As hybridizers pay attention to the plaintive plea of the average gardener for "more fragrance" doubtless the Musks and their descendants, the Noisettes, will concern them.

Evergreen Rose (Rosa sempervirens)

To be evergreen is another need of the *perfect* Climbing Rose. The climbing or trailing *Rosa sempervirens,* the Evergreen Rose of the Mediterranean, has thin, flexible canes, and large, single, fragrant, white flowers borne in June and early July. In a mild winter, or in the South, leaves remain the greater part of the year. Hybrids were produced in France around 1825, but few are available here today.

Whence Repeated Bloom?

Until the advent of Blaze and New Dawn, there were few true climbers of reliable recurrent or everblooming tendency for the North. In the South, the Noisettes repeat their great surges of color. Constant flowering and vegetative growth are not easily combined elements, however, and few of the species we have been discussing repeat in the wild. If they do, the habit is rarely carried over when plants are grown under conditions less ideal for them. *Rosa moschata* can be remontant, and the Noisettes reflect this tendency and also that of their other remontant parent, *R. chinensis,* the Bengal or China Rose. The character of rebloom, however, is recessive so hybridizers in making crosses have tried to repeat the quality by utilizing more than one rose with chinensis blood.

The Bengal or China Rose produces 2-inch, crimson or pink flowers, rarely paler ones, and the blooms deepen rather than fade as they age. This is a valuable trait since no gardener enjoys a flaming red rose whose passing covers his house for days with "blued" crimson blossoms. In *R. chinensis mutabilis*, there is an apparent change of color as the relative strengths of the sulphur-yellow and red are altered and the spent rose deepens to crimson. The foliage of the Chinas tends to be evergreen. Climbing sports were produced by *R. chinensis* but they are not to be had today.

A close relative of *Rosa chinensis*, and doubtless descended from a common ancestor, is *R. odorata*, also from China. It is called the Tea Rose because the fragrance of its flowers resembles that of crushed, *fresh* tea leaves. Flowers look like the chinensis, but they are larger and more fragrant and in pale shades of pink and yellow, and also white. Plants are tender except in the South where the long summers and gradual changes of climate approximate those of the native land of the Tea Rose. Immune to mildew and rarely subject to blackspot, plants are long-lived as well as everblooming. The Climbing Teas are indeed among the loveliest of the tall roses, treasured wherever it is possible to grow them. The notably hardy Gloire de Dijon may belong here; others of the class are Belle Portugaise *(R. odorata gigantea* hybrid), Belle Lyonnaise, Climbing Devoniensis, Climbing Maman Cochet, and Ruth Vestal.

If you try to grow the Climbing Teas in a northern garden, you will have to give particular attention to winter protection, applying and removing coverings gradually.

Many other species have contributed in various ways to our modern Climbing Roses. The flesh-colored Climbing Souvenir de la Malmaison, fragrant and marvelous in spring, and the exquisite, very fragrant, rose-red-on-white Zephirine Drouhin, which repeats occasionally, represent *Rosa borbon-*

iana, the Bourbon Rose. White Banksia and Yellow Banksia are forms of a Chinese species *(R. Banksiae)* that flourish in southern gardens. Mermaid, one of the loveliest climbers ever produced, is a *R. bracteata* hybrid. The Cherokee Rose *(R. laevigata),* now naturalized in the south-eastern states, is of Chinese derivation. The trailing or climbing plants, which in Florida will attain 50 feet, produce in May or June large, white, single flowers with fluffy golden stamens. They are fragrant, a lovely addition to any countryside. *R. laevigata's* illustrious descendant is Silver Moon.

Then there are the tall hybrids of *Rosa rugosa*—Conrad Ferdinand Meyer, Nova Zembla, and others, also the beautiful creeping Max Graf. But of these various groups we shall have more to say later.

As we now simply glance at the species, we realize that Nature offers every element necessary for the creation of the perfect Climbing Rose. It has been the hybridizer's task to discover, emphasize, and recombine traits. The past twenty years have shown tremendous progress. Doubtless in ten years more, many favorites of today will be outmoded! Probably only everbloomers will be introduced, and Silver Moon, American Climber, and Dorothy Perkins will become "collector's items" and belong to history.

CHAPTER THREE

Classifying the Climbers

VARIOUS SYSTEMS have been devised for classifying Climbing Roses, but they don't classify too easily, being plants of complicated ancestry and variable habit. If you attempt an hereditary classification, as *Multifloras, Setigeras, Wichuraianas,* you run into the fact that the life lines have been considerably mingled. If you divide them into Hardy and Tender groups, you discover you must be very arbitrary: the supposedly tender Mermaid often thrives in cold climates, and Gloire de Dijon flourishes in other than southern gardens. Healthy endurance of low temperature is only partly inherent; environment, culture, degree of exposure are also factors.

Climber, Rambler, or Pillar?

Attempts have also been made to classify the "tall" roses as Climbers, Ramblers, or Pillars. But what a mire of confusion we sink into there, some of the most familiar plants having been so curiously misnamed. Thus old Crimson

9. *Upper left:* Aloha, a fragrant pink Climbing Hybrid Tea. *(Courtesy, Jackson & Perkins).* 10. *Upper right:* Climbing Chrysler Imperial, a dark red Climbing Hybrid Tea. *(Courtesy, Germain's).* 11. *Lower left:* City of York, a white and rampant Large-flowered climber. *(Roche, Photo).* 12. *Lower right:* Coral Dawn, a fragrant, rose-pink Climbing Hybrid Tea. *(Courtesy, Jackson & Perkins).*

13. *Upper left:* Dream Girl, a spicily-fragrant, salmon-pink Large-flowered climber. *(Roche, Photo)*. 14. *Upper right:* Descanso Pillar, a rosy-red upright grower. *(Courtesy, Germain's)*. 15. *Lower left:* Dr. Huey, dark red and exuberant, excellent to cover a house wall. *(McFarland, Photo)*. 16. *Lower right:* Elegance, tall-growing and very hardy, one of the best yellows. *(McFarland, Photo)*.

17. *Upper left:* Inspiration, a fragrant, pink rose of moderate growth. *(Roche, Photo).* 18. *Upper right:* Mary Wallace, an old-time, rose-colored favorite among the once-bloomers. *(Roche, Photo).* 19. *Lower left:* Golden Climber (Mrs. Arthur Curtiss James), my cherished yellow, rampant and handsome. *(Roche, Photo).* 20. *Lower right:* Mrs. Whitman Cross, an orange-apricot Climbing Hybrid Tea. *(Roche, Photo).*

21. *Upper left:* Parade, carmine-pink, spicily-fragrant and reliably recurrent. *(Courtesy, Jackson & Perkins)*. 22. *Upper right:* Pink Cloud, lovely as its name, profuse and recurrent. *(Courtesy, Jackson & Perkins)*. 23. *Lower left:* Seven Sisters "with seven pink-to-crimson tints," introduced in 1817, still worth growing. *(McFarland, Photo)*. 24. *Lower right:* Red Flare, brilliant in June and August. *(Courtesy, Jackson & Perkins)*.

25. Mermaid, a choice, cream-yellow, single *Hybrid bracteata*, often hardy. *(Catherine Hemingway Smith, Arrangement; Roche, Photo)*

26. Climbing Dainty Bess with wild-rose beauty, charming for a basket. *(Margaret Carrick, Arrangement and Photo)*

27. Chevy Chase, a fragrant, crimson rose, outstanding among Ramblers. *(Roche, Photo)*

28. Little Compton Creeper, a single, deep-rose pink, charming for a ground cover. *(Roche, Photo)*

Rambler doesn't ramble; it's a strong, rampant climber. Paul's Scarlet Climber is not a climber but a neat pillar rose. American Pillar, on the other hand, is a terrific grower in constant need of pruning and overhauling if confined to a pillar.

As far as the term pillar is concerned, I wish it had never been applied. It has led to so much confusion, and is still being interpreted in new ways. Originally it meant roses of a type suited to pole-or pillar-growing; in maturity, not too tall. But now Mr. Brownell has called his new group of climbers Everblooming Pillars. Some of them go to 15 feet which is way beyond my idea of pillar growth. It seems to me that 8 feet is about as high as a pillar is ornamental.

My own idea of a pillar rose is still one suited to a pole— or a not-too-high trellis—a rose not overly tall-growing, or rampant, or bushy, so that it requires constant pruning. I would never try to fit New Dawn, City of York, or Thor to life on a pillar, but I would consider suitable for it the Climbing Hybrid Teas and other climbers like Dream Girl, Inspiration, or Prosperity. Also I feel a rose for pillar-growing should flower toe-to-top, even though canes are upright, which some climbers won't consider, insisting, as they do, on flowering only when grown horizontally, as Golden Climber.

Obviously, then, classification by growth-habit is too difficult. Furthermore, many climbers are so accommodating they will grow almost any way, even as bushes, and then there are the so-called Shrub Roses like Oratam and Skyrocket which readily climb if supported. I think of them as Could-Be Climbers, and include with these for low trellises or fence-growing certain of the adaptable Musks, Rugosas, Noisettes, Hybrid Perpetuals, and trailers, too. Even the designation of "climber" must be arbitrary, as we have already pointed out.

Once- or Repeat-blooming

So we come back to the flower itself, and most importantly to the span of its appearance. Now that there are so many more recurrent or everblooming types than there were, major classifications of Once-blooming and Repeat-blooming seem sensible. Within these broad divisions, we can indicate size of flower: "large," 2 inches or more; "small," less than 2 inches, the border line cases being given the benefit of the doubt. We can also indicate *something* of flower form, as Climbing Hybrid Tea, etc.

Because fragrance is so important to me, I considered for a time broad subdivisions under Once-blooming and Repeat-blooming of Fragrant and Non-fragrant, but such divisions made me feel guilty. I seemed to be applying an unpleasant label, Non-fragrant, to many fine varieties, such as Paul's Scarlet. I therefore decided such information should be reserved for the varietal descriptions.

Once-blooming and Recurrent or Repeat-blooming, also Everblooming, are all terms for interpretation. Recurrent or Repeat-blooming means at least occasional flowering during summer and a good show in September; at best, there are always a few flowers. Everblooming indicates a pretty fair showing all the time—the aim of most hybridizers. Periods of bloom vary not only with varieties but with the same varieties under different conditions. In particularly favorable locations, as in the South or on the West Coast, Tausendschön may bloom sporadically all season while in the East it will flower only in June. Also, Silver Moon flowers rather briefly for only about three weeks, but Thor for six, both being primarily Once-bloomers, however.

As for Everblooming, that is a big order. The hybridizer has been hard put to it to give to one plant the power to grow tall and also to bloom continuously. Most climbers bloom on old wood. New flowering stems come from the year-old or older canes. If, when faded, the first blooms are cut off, new flowers develop just beneath them. This practice encourages the everblooming habit and is followed with all the repeaters except the Hybrid Teas. These throw up canes which flower the same season they appear, so also do many of the newer climbers and newer Shrub Roses. The Brownell Everblooming Pillars set no blind canes; they flower on wood of the current season. Break a branch anywhere and a *flowering* stem is immediately produced. Only let these plants develop a vast frame—which will be winter-hardy—and they will keep pretty well covered with long-stemmed flowers.

Climbing Hybrid Teas and Floribundas are constant flower-producers but not in vast quantities, though more on the latter than on the former, but both are moderate growers and slow. When a delicate environmental balance is achieved, plants bloom satisfactorily while also steadily growing tall.

Blaze and New Dawn operate differently. They grow considerably, New Dawn being more rampant than Blaze. Then they stop and cover themselves with glory, repeating the process the season through. New Dawn is a sport of Dr. W. Van Fleet, also a mighty grower; Blaze, the result of a cross between Paul's Scarlet Climber and the Hybrid Tea, Gruss an Teplitz.

Source of Climbers

Many climbers have originated as sports or bud mutations of bush varieties of Teas, Hybrid Teas, Floribundas or Polyanthas; but a few have originated as seedlings of bush types. Sports are spontaneous variations. A single *long* shoot develops on a bush, and this can be propagated. The new plants retain the flower color and form of the original bush variety but have an entirely different habit of growth. Instead of staying dwarf, they produce long, vigorous canes which behave like those of other types of climbers. Although they are classed as repeat-blooming types, some do not seem to give as continuous a performance as their bush counterparts. They bloom freely in spring, produce a few flowers through the summer, and then perhaps give a good show in the fall. While they are growing through the summer, I suppose they should hardly be expected to give the quantity of bloom that appears in the spring, though some, like Climbing Crimson Glory, will usually do so. In the main, growing tall limits flowering.

Incidentally, and I think this is news, I saw a plant of Silver Moon which recently produced a branch that flowered repeatedly through the summer although the main plant ceased to produce after the usual season. Unfortunately the repeating branch was improperly layered and so was winter-killed. However, the parent plant is being closely observed, and it is hoped another repeat-blooming branch will appear and prove possible of propagation. This is an example of another type of mutation.

The Climbing Teas, Hybrid Teas, Floribundas, and Noisettes are well adapted to California, the South, and other milder sections of the country where temperatures do not usually go to zero. This is only a general remark, however, because some are being successfully grown where temperatures do drop below zero. I think, for instance, of Gloire de Dijon which does well in some northern gardens.

Useful Symbols

But to return to the matter of classification, I think you will find this rather new approach useful—and usable—not

too arbitrary, but indicative of many broad divisions of roses
that belong in the category of climbers. Groups are referred
to by the commonly-used symbols, but perhaps we should add
a new one, Tr for trailers, since these are rather a definite
group.

Alp	Alpina	HC	Hyb. China
Arv	Arvensis	HD	Hyb. Damask
B	Bourbon	HEglanteria	Hyb.
C	China		Eglanteria
CB	Climbing	HFt	Hyb. Foetida
	Bourbon	HG	Hyb. Gigantea
CC	Cl. China	HLaev	Hyb. Laevigata
Cent	Centifolia	HMs	Hyb. Moschata
CFl	Cl. Floribunda	HNut	Hyb. Nutkana
CHG	Cl. Hyb.	HP	Hyb. Perpetual
	Gigantea	HRug	Hyb. Rugosa
CHP	Cl. Hybrid	HSet	Hyb. Setigera
	Perpetual	HSpn	H. Spinosissima
CHT	Cl. Hyb. Tea	HT	Hyb. Tea
Cl	Climber	HWich	Hyb.
CPol	Cl. Polyantha		Wichuraiana
CT	Cl. Tea	LC	Large-flowered
D	Damask		Climber
Evbl.Semi-Cl.	Everblooming	M	Moss
	Semi-	N	Noisette
	Climber	R	Rambler
HAlba	Hyb. Alba	Rug	Rugosa
H.Arv.Cl.	Hyb. Arvensis	Semi-Cl	Semi-Climber
	Climber	Spn	Spinosissima
HB	Hyb. Bourbon	T	Tea
HBc	Hyb. Bracteata	Tr	Trailer

CLASSIFICATION FOR CLIMBERS AND COULD-BE CLIMBERS

Once-blooming

Large-flowered (LC)—Paul's Scarlet
Small-flowered—Ramblers (R) —Chevy Chase
Tall-Shrub Types
    Eglanteria Hybrids (HEglanteria) —Lady Penzance
    Spinosissima Hybrids (HSpn)—Spring Gold
Trailers (Tr)—Coral Creeper

Repeat-blooming

Large-flowered (LC)—New Dawn—Brownell Everblooming Pillars
Climbing Hybrid Teas (CHT) —Cl. Christopher Stone
Climbing Floribundas (CFl) —Cl. Goldilocks
Hybrid Perpetuals (HP)—Frau Karl Druschki
Tall-Shrub Types
    Hybrid Musks (HMs)—Pemberton Pillars—Cornelia
    Hybrid Rugosas (HRug)—Sarah Van Fleet
    Hybrid Noisettes (HN) —Cl. Gloire de Dijon
    Hybrid Modern Shrubs (Shrub) —Fragrant Beauty
Trailers (Tr)—Creeping Everbloom

In addition to the classifications, you should know something about quality of plants and type of understock before you order. For goodness' sake don't buy bargain roses. A good rose is inexpensive enough, and you don't want the bother of planting something that won't live—or won't thrive if it does live—or won't turn out to be the variety you ordered. The best grade, non-patented rose costs about $1.25 to $1.50; a patented variety, $1.50 to $3.00. (Patented roses are no better than others. The extra cost simply covers the *fair* royalty paid by the propagator to the owner of a patent on a variety. He may be the originator, or, as is more likely, the one who bought the originator's rights to the rose he "made.")

Grading of Roses

Officially a No. 1 grade rose has 3 to 5 canes and a root system in proportion to the top; a No. 1½, 2 canes; a No. 2 but one. What you want are two-year, field-grown, budded plants of No. 1 quality, not No. 2 grade or culls. And from growers of the good reputation of those listed on page 198 ff., you will doubtless receive only first-quality plants.

It doesn't make too much difference where your roses come from. Packing is so expert today, a journey does no damage. Usually it's more convenient to buy locally, though not always so, and, if a nearby section is swamped with orders at the time *you* want to plant, as the East in spring, it could be plants from a distance will reach you more promptly because the far-away nursery is not then so busy. Furthermore, the man who sells is not necessarily the man who grows. Maybe in New York you will buy roses that were grown in California or Texas—and it won't matter.

About Understocks

Type of understock can be an important factor in your success with climbers. The understock is the hardy (usually multiflora) base on which cuttings of more delicate constitution are budded. The point of union appears like a knob just above the roots. The method is, in spring, to insert an "eye" from a flowering shoot of a Climbing Hybrid Tea, say, into a slit in the bark of a plant of multiflora understock. The eye is held in place by an elastic strip. The next spring, the multiflora top growth is cut off just a quarter-inch above the eye. This little eye then makes a fine "two-year-old" plant by November of the second year.

Rosa multiflora is the most common understock in eastern

nurseries and in Texas, though Texas Wax is popular there also. In California, Ragged Robin or Shafter (Dr. Huey) is often used. Dorothy Perkins and American Pillar have also been tried.

In the South, *Rosa odorata* is a favorite. This, being tender, is not a proper understock for roses which are to be planted in the North, but a southern grower would hardly supply a northern customer with odorata stock. However, odorata is right for the Deep South, also Ragged Robin. Conversely, roses on multiflora do not always live there, which is understandable in view of multiflora's habitat. Multiflora does make a fine branching root system which thrives almost everywhere else.

A number of multiflora forms have also been used with more or less success as understocks—*carnea, cathayensis, Chenault* 5892, and *polyantha*—also *Rosa moschata floribunda* and *R. setigera*. This whole important matter of understocks is now under further investigation at the Iowa Agricultural Experiment Station at Ames, another example of the serious interest in this most popular of all ornamentals —the rose.

1. Pink Climbing Roses outline the pleasant architectural lines of a Cape Cod cottage, accent the doorway, and grow in riotous profusion over the fence. *(Genereux, Photo)*

2. Blaze on a lamppost repeats its glory every month. *(Genereux, Photo)*

3. New Dawn produces spring-to-autumn loveliness beside a wellhead. *(Genereux, Photo)*

FOUR
MARVELOUS
VARIETIES

4. *Above,* Brownell's Everblooming Pillar, No. 84, an everblooming yellow of great excellence. *(Genereux, Photo)*

5. *Left,* the fragrant pink Aloha, a Climbing Hybrid Tea, that blooms the season through. *(Genereux, Photo)*

6. *Above,* Brownell's Everblooming Pillar, No. 73, an outstanding introduction which flowers continuously top to toe *(Genereux, Photo)*

7. *Right,* Climbing Goldilocks, a polyantha of steady bloom. *(McFarland, Photo)*

8. Climbing Roses—the fragrant pink Dr. J. H. Nicolas, scarlet Blaze, and in the background, white-centered American Pillar —make a handsome background for a garden with bushes of Pink Bountiful and Red Pinocchio in foreground. *(Genereux, Photo)*

9. Like fire along a fence, Paul's Scarlet, almost unattended, blooms in brilliant beauty. *(Genereux, Photo)*

10. Over a garden wall, Coral Creeper, a charming trailer, opens clusters of fragrant, single, pink flowers of wild-rose appeal. *(Genereux, Photo)*

CHAPTER ☙ FOUR

The Choice Is Yours

IF YOU HAVE ROOM for only a few climbers, what a hard time you are going to have making a selection. Today there are some 300 available, the more popular ones like Blaze, Climbing Crimson Glory, Climbing Goldilocks, New Dawn, Paul's Scarlet Climber, and Silver Moon, to be had almost everywhere; some fine but not-so-well-known ones offered less generally. The number of really reliable, handsome, satisfactory varieties is, however, legion, and I was hard put to it to limit myself to the list of 75 Excellent Climbers which follows near the end of this chapter.

On the whole, these 75 varieties will grow almost anywhere in this country, except perhaps in the *Deep* South. Indeed, you will find if you compare lists of favorite and successful varieties made up by enthusiasts in, say, California, Ohio, and New York that there is pretty general agreement. Too much stress is laid, I think, on special roses for special climates, and on peculiar methods for supposedly "difficult" areas. In general, the *timing* of operations of planting, spraying, and pruning varies but not the method. The necessity for winter protection is also *not* nationwide. Furthermore,

∾᪄᪄ 41

in some favored warmer regions, as the Deep South, it is possible to enjoy a wider range of types and varieties. There emphasis may well be on the Climbing Teas and Noisettes, and certain of the more tender Climbing Hybrid Teas. For this area choice is better made from Best Climbers for the South at the end of this chapter.

Of course, I have omitted some of *your* favorites, and that can't be helped. Who can be objective about anything so personally appealing as a rose? *My* affections are bound to be reflected here, though I have included Climbing Peace, which is not among my favorites. I cannot really like it. Reports indicate it is a variable producer, and I think it is so over-large it lacks refinement, and there is little compensating fragrance. Still it *is* popular. I *have* included that dark-pink, cabbagy bloomer, Reichspräsident von Hindenburg, though it is rare, but I would always choose it for its marvelously sweet fragrance, and grow this supposedly bush Hybrid Tea as a climber. And then for fragrance, there is Mercedes Gallart, which I rather like though one eminent rosarian says it "has everything but beauty." But many of the older Van Fleet varieties are not here, like Bess Lovett and Alida Lovett; also some introductions seemed too new for a basic list though I feel sure Climbing Chrysler Imperial and Climbing Red Flare will make their mark!

But many of the old and somewhat-newer varieties are among those present. Some of the once-bloomers are still worth growing for their beauty, coverage, hardiness, fragrance in some cases, and suitability to areas of serious Japanese beetle infestation where repeat-bloomers are no joy. Elsewhere I suppose we all incline to want more than June or June-into-July bloom, so we may prefer an Aloha to a Mary Wallace, a yellow Brownell Everblooming Pillar to a Golden Climber, however much we have favored the latter in the past. So I could go on, explaining each inclusion, defending each omission. Really, selecting only 75 Climbing Roses is a frustrating business. But if you let *your* choice lie among them, I think you will be pleased.

The Brownell Everblooming Pillars

Had these newest pillar roses been named, they would certainly have found place among the 75 Excellent Climbers, for I cannot too strongly recommend them. Blooms are large, to 3½ or 4 inches, and double (25 to 40 petals), colors clear, and in a broad range of hues. The plants have real pest-and-disease resistance, and will stand 15 degrees below zero without protection. In four years, they climb 10 to 15 feet. Flowers cover plants from the first year on—and no blind canes are produced. In the portfolio of color you can see them in Plates 4 and 6, also in Photograph 57. Brownell Everblooming Pillars are big news in Climbing Roses. This is the line up:

No. 104—the true dark red
No. 73—excellent deep-rose
No. 82—dark, high-centered, salmon-pink, Hybrid-Tea form
No. 83—lovely, very-double salmon-pink
No. 84—well-formed golden-yellow
No. 122—cream-yellow, form uninteresting
No. 126—another salmon-pink
No. 214—light yellow

75 EXCELLENT CLIMBERS

Ramblers are not included among the 75, nor the trailers. These have Chapter 5 to themselves, and those Shrub Roses which you can grow as climbers are separately discussed in Chapter 7.

Pink and Pink-to-Red Blends

Aloha (1949). CHT. Ovoid bud and very double, 3½-inch, salmon-pink flowers. A real beauty where it succeeds; in some climates and some seasons, it apparently has a tendency to ball, and blooms do open rather quickly. Long stems and handsome shining foliage. Grows 8 to 10 feet. Continuous bloom, but give it two to three years to establish. Usually better in cooler climates, but also very satisfactory in Florida. Wonderful tea FRAGRANCE. One of my favorites.

American Pillar (1908). LC. An old variety, indispensable among once-bloomers for late June. Immense clusters of single, carmine-pink, white-eyed flowers with prominent golden stamens. Long, strong stems and large, leathery, glossy leaves, which are almost evergreen. Handsome, enduring plants growing to 20 feet or more. Fall crop of red fruit is also very decorative.

Blossomtime (1951). Cl. Flesh-pink with salmon reverse, each petal neatly rolled back, superb Hybrid-Tea form, medium-sized and double. A restrained Semiclimber to 6 to 7 feet; fine for fence-growing or a pillar. Constant bloom. Excellent in Florida, too. Dependable, lovely, with tea FRAGRANCE.

Cl. American Beauty (1909). LC. An old June favorite and still popular, though the cerise flowers do blue with age. Very large, cupped blooms on long stems. Vigorous climber to 12 to 15 feet. Best grown in semishade to slow up fading. This is actually a Wichuraiana hybrid, and not a sport or climbing form of the bush American Beauty. Considered by some to be the most perfumed of roses, a sweet and heady damask FRAGRANCE.

Cl. Cécile Brunner (Sweetheart Rose) (1904). CFl. For those who cherish this plant of "a thousand exquisite pink buds" there is no substitute, although the tiny beauties open to rather shapeless, sometimes even "soiled-looking," small, double, pink-on-yellow flowers in clusters. Faithful June-into-August bloom. Sparse, soft, light foliage, and growth to 10 or more feet; will cover a garage at the seashore, and is nice there and also in the South, planted with Cl. Yellow Cécile Brunner. Slight tea FRAGRANCE.

Cl. Dainty Bess (1935). CHT. For all who love single flowers, this is a darling. Pointed buds and dainty, wild-rose pink, 3½- to 4-inch flowers with wine-colored stamens and 5 broad, fringed petals. Exquisite for flower arrangements. Heavy resistant foliage and vigorous climbing form to 8 to 10 feet.

Cl. Picture (1942). CHT. Among the most reliable of the CHT's. Clear, light-pink, double (34 reflexed petals), high-centered flowers, profuse and everblooming, considered by some to be even better than the bush form in size of flower and performance of plant. Dark, glossy foliage. Good grower to 9 feet. Slightly FRAGRANT.

Cl. Pinkie (1952). CFl. Large clusters of semidouble, 1¾- to 2½-inch, rose-colored, cupped flowers in wonderful and constant profusion. (Nice with Cl. Goldilocks and

Cl. Summer Snow; for landscape effect rather than picking.) Soft, glossy foliage. Vigorous to 8 to 9 feet. A real charmer everywhere and much grown on the West Coast and in the South, excellent in Florida. Slightly FRAGRANT.

Cl. Pinocchio (1951). CFl. Long sprays of pink, salmon-suffused, 2-inch, double, cupped flowers. Everblooming in the manner of the bush Floribunda. Pleasing color combination with Cl. Goldilocks of same type. Leathery, resistant foliage. Vigorous to 7 to 8 feet. Fruity FRAGRANCE.

Cl. Radiance (1928). CHT. Globular buds and large, rather double, cupped, rose-pink flowers, lighter on the petal reverses, open to not-so-distinguished flowers as those of some Hybrid Teas, but the Radiance group, which includes Red Radiance and the salmon-pink Mrs. Charles Bell, has set "a standard of dependability" among Hybrid Teas. Hardy, and grows 10 to 12 feet. Very FRAGRANT.

Cl. Santa Anita (1946). CHT. Long, pointed buds; 3½- to 4-inch, semidouble (20 to 23 petals), high-centered, peach-pink flowers. Profuse, recurrent bloom. Light foliage. Sturdy climber to 8 to 12 feet. Highly rated among CHT's of this type.

Cl. Show Girl (1949). CHT. Huge, urn-shaped bud; deep-pink, semidouble (15 to 20 petals), 3½- to 4½-inch, cupped flowers on long stems. One of the best of the CHT's. Vigorous grower to 12 feet. Healthy, profuse, and FRAGRANT.

Cl. Souvenir de la Malmaison (1943). CB. Among the very choicest of the old-fashioned roses. Huge, double, pale-pink blooms, cupped and quartered, appear in a great spring mass covering the plant from top to bottom, a little smaller perhaps than those on the bush counterpart, and there is no comparable repeat of bloom. It grows to 20 feet and is among the hardiest of Bourbons, excellent in the South, and with fine, damask FRA-GRANCE.

Coral Dawn (1952). Cl. Pointed buds and double, 4½-inch, coral-pink flowers that do not fade; as continuous a bloomer as New Dawn, and flowers have more distinction, I think. Truly magnificent where I have seen it. Resistant dark-green foliage. Vigorous grower to 8 to 12 feet. FRAGRANT.

Coral Pillar (1945). CHT. Enormous, high-centered, superb yellow-flame-coral blend of marvelous form. Constant bloom. Large, dark, glossy foliage. Of varying vigor from 10 to 20 feet (at seashore 10 feet in a summer), excellent upright grower. Very FRAGRANT.

Descanso (1952). Shrub. Urn-shaped buds; coral-to-scarlet, 4½- to 5-inch, double (30- to 35-petaled), high-centered flowers with scalloped edges. Very long stems. Recurrent bloom. Large, glossy, dark leaves on 6- to 7-foot plants. Also called Descanso Pillar.

Dream Girl (1944). LC. Large (3½-inch), double (55-65 petals), unfading, pale coral-pink flowers. Starts to bloom late in June when many other climbers are resting. Recurrent, but sometimes temperamental. Glossy, dark green, resistant foliage. Vigorous, though slow, climber to 8 to 11 feet. Excellent for pillars, and very hardy. Spicy FRAGRANCE, but *not always noticeable*.

Dr. J. H. Nicolas (1940). LC. "Age cannot wither, nor custom stale" this superb rose-pink climber of dependable recurrent bloom. Very double, 5- to 6-inch flowers in clusters of 3 or 4, of old-fashioned Hybrid Perpetual form—sumptuous! This rose is a fine producer, even first-year plants do well if you cut blossoms with stems only to first true leaf. Dark leathery foliage and vigor-

ous, but rather slow, pillar growth to 8 feet, nice for a
front-door trellis. Very FRAGRANT. Tops with me!

Ednah Thomas (formerly Bloomfield Improvement) (1931).
CHT. Large, double, rich salmon-rose, exhibition-quality blooms, several in a cluster on long, strong stems.
Recurrent bloom. Reaches 12 feet, and, if killed to
ground, will grow up again vigorously. Hardiness depends on rootstock, Texas Wax probably better than
multiflora for this one. Semihardy in Philadelphia area.
Marvelous FRAGRANCE.

Inspiration (1946). LC. Two-toned, peach-pink, of excellent,
semidouble, Hybrid-Tea form, opening slowly. Keeps
its looks for a longer time than flowers of many newer
varieties; unbelievably heavy June-through-October
crop, grand for cutting. Rampant to 10 to 12 feet, but
give it three years to get there. Along a fence, every
15-inch stem will grow upright; also good on trellis or
pillar. Large glossy foliage. Always some bloom. Same
type flower as Dream Girl, and more dependable. Strong
tea FRAGRANCE.

Kitty Kininmonth (1922). HG. Very large, loose, cupped,
semidouble, deep-pink, almost-fadeless blooms, with
prominent golden stamens. "A show-stopper in spring"
and a practically foolproof plant to 12 feet. Dark
wrinkled foliage, few thorns. Heavy June bloom the
full length of the canes, sparingly repeated. Slight
FRAGRANCE.

Mary Wallace (1924). LC. One of the wonderful Van Fleet
climbers that still draws you to it in any rose garden.
"Planted thirty years ago, has had a minimum of care,
still lovely," or the "feature of our nursery display" are
comments I still hear on M.W. Long, pointed buds;
very large, semidouble, cupped flowers of warm rose-
pink, heavy in June, also some in summer and fall.

Glossy, rich-green foliage. Vigorous, almost rank, 8- to 12-foot growth. Very hardy. Slight FRAGRANCE. Completely reliable in every way, meant for have-but-don't-do gardeners.

May Queen (1898). HW. Lilac-pink, semidouble, short-stemmed, 3-inch flowers in garland effect. This will do well in almost complete shade provided this is open, as on the north side of a house. Good glossy foliage. Plant grows to at least 30 feet and tends to bloom all season. On West Coast *does* so after a great May profusion. Strong, sweet FRAGRANCE.

Mme. Grégoire Staechelin (Spanish Beauty) (1929). LC. Huge, open, semidouble, ruffled, delicate-pink blossoms, stained crimson. Earlier than most climbers, producing abundant late May and early June bloom. Long stems; heavy, dark, resistant foliage. Vigorous grower to 14 feet. An outstanding climber among once-bloomers. Slight FRAGRANCE.

New Dawn (1930). LC. This rose never disappointed anyone! Exquisite from pointed bud to double, 4-inch Hybrid-Tea type blooms, blush-pink. Lovely for arrangements. Dependably recurrent. Long stems; dark, glossy foliage and real vigor to 20 feet. (Same as Van Fleet, but recurrent.) One plant gives tremendous display. A let-alone grower, extremely hardy in all regions. Beautiful with turquoise-blue or gray-green furnishings or house trim; pleasant associated with Virginia creeper. Charming with blue delphinium and single white peonies. Slightly FRAGRANT "close to nose." Obviously —one of my favorites.

Parade (1953). LC. Outstanding among deep pink or rose-red climbers—dependably recurrent, heavy spring and fall bloom, intermittent between. Wonderful clarity of color. Ovoid bud; double, 4-inch, cupped, lasting flowers on long stems. Dark-green, resistant foliage. Vigorous 8-foot plants, producing many new flowering canes in summer. Blooms the first year. Grows well in semi-shade which preserves deep coloring. Fine spicy FRAGRANCE. Among rich pinks, I do like this one.

Pink Cloud (1952). LC. Ovoid buds; large clusters of 3½-inch flowers of a delectable, delicate, pale, true-pink (deeper than blush), from spring into late summer. Really pretty as a cloud, and blooms even the first year. Shiny, disease-resistant foliage. Grows 6 to 8 feet, excellent upright bloomer, but also good on fences.

Reichspräsident von Hindenburg (1933). HT. This one really *is* a climber, but it is commonly described simply as HT, and it *looks* like an HP. If you have ever seen it, however, you know why I long to encourage its reappearance on growers' lists. It has big (6-inch) cabbagy, pink flowers, fully double and cupped. A wonderful crop in spring, in July, and again dependably in September. Vigorous grower to 8 to 10 feet, of undeniable effective color. And what FRAGRANCE, noticeable even from afar! Intense!

Temptation (1950). LC. Ovoid bud; loose, rumpled, large, double (40-petal) bloom in ever-changing hues from spring to fall—deep lavender-pink, to flesh-pink, to rose-red in autumn; constant bloom. Large, glossy foliage. Vigorous pillar growth (average 6½ feet), but possibly to 12 feet in five years; nice performer even first year. Among the very best.

Wind Chimes. HMs. Clusters of small, single deep-pink flowers in the shade, lighter in full sun followed by round orange fruits "like little doorknobs." In constant bloom, this is choice, with all the vigor, pest- and disease-resistance, and wonderful musky sweetness of its family. (Only available from Tillotson, I think.) FRAGRANT.

Zephirine Drouhin (1868). B. Long, pointed buds; large, semidouble, shapely, cerise-pink flowers borne in spring and at later intervals, some in fall. Very hardy Semi-climber to 8 to 10 feet. Exquisite FRAGRANCE.

Red

Blaze (1932). LC. Probably the most brilliant of the reds. Newer strains are truly everblooming June through September. (Stock has varied considerably in production.) Large clusters of 2- to 3-inch, semidouble, cupped flowers. Large, leathery, resistant foliage. Vigorous plants 10 to 15 feet. Fine on pillar or fence, but a color not to overdo. Take time to nip out faded flowers. Unless you live in a bad beetle area and don't want summer bloom, plant this instead of Paul's Scarlet. Only slightly FRAGRANT.

Cl. Christopher Stone (1942). CHT. A fine, dependable red in this class, one of hardiest. Long, pointed bud; semidouble, 5-inch flowers are pure spectrum red with the sun shining through them. Bright green foliage. Excellent pillar rose to 12 to 15 feet. (More desirable than Scorcher.) Strong, heady FRAGRANCE, real old-rose scent.

Cl. Crimson Glory (1946). CHT. Fat, pointed buds; large, double (30 petals), ruby-velvet blooms with almost-black shadings, no bluing with age or fading in sunshine; much heavier bloomer than bush form; very long stems on first crop, successive blooms on shorter stems, and may have weak necks as bloom is heavy. Leathery foliage. Let it grow *upright* on arch, trellis, or pillar, or (as I have it), up a fence *post* and over a white pine tree. To 10 feet with 2-inch basal canes possible in six

years, but is well established in two years. Crops of
bloom through season, especially heavy in early fall,
with scattering of flowers in between. Among *hardiest*
of Climbing Hybrid Teas, also good in Florida. Don't
miss this one! Rich damask FRAGRANCE.

Cl. Etoile de Hollande (1931). CHT. Bright red, double
(35 to 45 petals), very large, cupped flowers. Color is
quite sun-resistant. Recurrent bloom. Soft foliage and
dependable climbing habit to 8 feet. This is very popular on the West Coast where it is sometimes described
as "the best red climber." Blooms are actually larger
(5 to 6 inches) than on bush form. Beautiful buds and
long stems, with plenty of bloom for cutting. Marvelous
old-rose FRAGRANCE.

Cl. Mme. Henri Guillot (1947). CHT. Coral-red blend
with exhibition-quality blooms and exceedingly handsome foliage. Vigorous to 6 feet and hardy without protection at Philadelphia. Only slight FRAGRANCE.

Cl. Red Duchess (1954). CHT. Long, pointed buds; 3½- to
5-inch double (50 petals), high-centered, translucent,
rich, rosy-red flowers. Reliably recurrent bloom. Long,
strong stems and glossy, resistant, bronzy foliage. Upright, bushy grower to 15 to 18 feet. Very hardy, even
to subzero. Better make the acquaintance of this striking beauty. Spicy FRAGRANCE.

Cl. Red Radiance (1929). CHT. As dependable as Cl. Pink
Radiance (above) and as FRAGRANT.

Dr. Huey (1920). LC. One of the most reliable for June
bloom. In any collection, you notice its floriferousness,
though other roses are certainly more beautiful. Semidouble, 2-inch, maroon flowers (darker than Crimson
Glory), that do not blue with age; prominent, light-
yellow stamens. Clusters of 3 or 4. Rich, green foliage.
Vigorous grower to 15 feet. Handsome espaliered

against a house. Very hardy and resistant, except for mildew if crowded; used as a leading California root-stock.

Mercedes Gallart (1932). CHT. Large, very double, crim-son-pink flowers changing to steady, bright crimson after midsummer. Not too distinguished form or color but good foliage and vigorous growth. Dependably remont-ant and hardy. Exceedingly fine damask FRAGRANCE.

Paul's Scarlet Climber (1916). LC. This is the profuse June-flowering climber that covers the East. Flowers are medium-sized, semidouble, scarlet, in large clusters of 7 to 10. Color does not burn or fade unpleasantly. The much-branched canes are flexible, easily tied to a fence or trellis, rampant enough to cover a pergola or grow on an arbor. Extend perhaps to 12 feet. Blaze is a recurrent hybrid of Paul's Scarlet x Gruss an Teplitz. It covers less space, is as dependably hardy, usually pref-erable, except in areas where beetles are rampant. Neither Paul's Scarlet nor Blaze has much scent. (The former is often supplied as own-root plants.)

Skyrocket (called Wilhelm in Germany) (1934). Shrub. But what a nice climber it makes, too! Large trusses of as many as 75 semidouble, 2-inch, rich-crimson flowers, black-red in the bud. Outstanding in any garden, does not fade. Abundant and continuous flowering. Glossy, dark, blue-green leaves. Grows to 7 feet and is an eye-catcher. Excellent for pillar or trellis. The first time I saw it I walked the length of a long garden in the pour-ing rain to identify it. Skyrocket! What a perfect name for this explosion of color! Sweet honey FRAGRANCE. (If you can't locate it, get Eva which is similar but has a white center and looks more carmine than crimson.)

Sunday Best (1924). CHP. Important because it is one of the few single, everblooming climbers. Long, pointed bud; 3-inch, semidouble, ruffled flowers, vivid crimson to carmine with a white eye, richer coloring in partial shade. Starts to bloom early and goes right on even past a first light frost. Wrinkled foliage, not too attractive. Hardy to zero anyway. It appears to me, though, it should branch more, great long canes springing from base are garlanded the entire length with bloom. Grows to 8 to 10 feet.

Thor (1940). LC. Ovoid bud and 4- to 6-inch very double, dark-red flowers (rather like Crimson Glory). They open slowly and do not discolor with age. Plant this on your house and near a much-used door for six weeks of scent and beauty, starting late May. Foot-long stems on vigorous plants 10 to 30 feet, even in some cold climates, and without protection. Large, leathery, truly-resistant foliage. There is nothing to touch Thor among dark reds, but it *is* a once-bloomer, though over a long period. Needs protection in some colder regions but all Thors seem variable as to height and cold-tolerance. In Philadelphia, Thor develops a trunk as big as a well-grown peach tree. Rich damask FRAGRANCE. I love it!

White

City of York (1945). LC. Creamy-white, 3-inch, semidouble, cupped flowers in clusters of 7 to 15. Opens wide to show prominent golden stamens. Pretty with a yellow climber. Profuse once-bloomer; in California may bloom in fall too. Dark, lustrous, resistant foliage. Very vigorous to 8 to 15 feet, and hardy. Everybody likes this handsome white climber. Robert Pyle, who gave it to my friend, Mrs. Lewis M. Hull, in whose garden I first saw it, called it the "finest climber in a lifetime." Voted one of Six Best by Cincinnati Rose Society. Generally considered superior to Silver Moon. This newer white is really a beauty. FRAGRANT.

Cl. Snowbird (1947). CT. Exquisite buds, large, very double, high-centered white flowers, tinged lemon-yellow. Leathery foliage and very vigorous. Blooms dependably all season. Essentially for mild climates, as the South, though possibly hardy to Philadelphia. (Often classified as CHT, but not so.) Heavy tea FRAGRANCE, *even in the wood.*

Cl. Summer Snow (1936). CFl. Large clusters of 2-inch, semidouble, cupped flowers from July into October. Not the distinction of Hybrid-Tea Climbers, but what dependability and effectiveness, especially on a garden arch or with growth flung over a pine tree. For take-it-easy gardeners, the Climbing Floribundas are tops. This with Cl. Goldilocks and Cl. Pinocchio or Cl. Pinkie makes a nice color range. Vigorous grower to 8 to 10 feet. Slightly FRAGRANT.

Frau Karl Druschki (1901). HP. One of the handsomest of all snow-white roses. Buds are pointed and tinged carmine pink. Profuse bloom in May and June. Cut it back to encourage rebloom in autumn. Foliage is large and dark. Bush is a vigorous grower to 7 feet on a fence. It's against my principles to be very enthusiastic about any but fragrant roses and this *is* scentless. But *you* grow it as a climber and see if you aren't full of praise, too!

Glenn Dale (1927). LC. One of the wonderful once-blooming Van Fleet roses, among the finest of the white climbers. Graceful ivory buds; large, very double (30 to 50 petals), snow-white flowers in great clusters on long, strong stems. Dark, leathery, resistant foliage. Grows to 10 feet, an excellent pillar rose, and very hardy.

Kathleen (1922). HMs. This is healthy and hardy in sun or shade, will grow up to 15 feet, bringing delicious scent to you at second-story windows, or will stop lower down and be shrubby. In constant bloom, it looks like a bough of apple blossoms, the small, single, white flowers, pink in the bud, appearing in long-stemmed clusters. Really FRAGRANT.

Mme. Alfred Carrière (1879). N. A very vigorous climber with large, double, cupped blooms opening blush. Can be depended upon to grow to at least 20 feet and to give intermittent flowers all season, with a second very large display in September. Hardy at Philadelphia with protection. Intensely FRAGRANT.

Paul's Lemon Pillar (1915). CHT. Pale-yellow buds; very large, velvety-white, full (about 23 petals), semidouble flowers of handsome Hybrid-Tea form. Rarely reblooms, so leave faded flowers and a fine crop of huge hips will follow. Shining, dark foliage but some blackspot. Vigorous to 15 feet. Hardy at Philadelphia with no protection although considered a rose primarily for the South. Tea FRAGRANCE.

Prosperity (1919). HMs. Great clusters of small, fully-double, pink-tinted, white flowers, opening from rosetted buds, on strong stems from June to frost. Makes neat bushy pillar growth to 8 feet, also fine to spread out on fence. If you want an *everblooming* white, look no further: this is a beauty. (Worthwhile, though in some seasons it will mildew somewhat.) FRAGRANT.

Silver Moon (1910). LC. Clusters of long, pointed, pale-yellow buds; large (4½-inch), semidouble, pure-white flowers with prominent golden stamens, suggesting the Cherokee parent. Profuse June bloom; lovely buds and blooms for cutting. Long, strong stems and glossy, dark, almost-evergreen, leathery foliage. Among finest of once-blooming white climbers, very vigorous to 25 to 30 feet; good effect by second year; best in full sun. Makes a strong "trunk"; also a tall, impenetrable hedge if given some top pruning. A recurrent-flowering Silver Moon is, as I have said, very much still a possibility. Slightly FRAGRANT.

White Dawn (1949). LC. This is a white climber with *recurrent* bloom, a much-needed type. Plant not so vigorous nor flowers so large as its counterpart, New Dawn, or the once-blooming City of York, but still an excellent grower to 8 feet; a profuse bloomer with a veritable snowfall of small white, double (35 petals), gardenia-like blooms in clusters in June, and reliably through season. Straight sturdy stems; glossy foliage.

White Gold (1943). LC. Bud long and pointed. Double, high-centered, white flowers with yellow centers and reflexed petals in profusion in June and July. Dark, glossy foliage. Vigorous growth to 20 feet, very hardy.

White Banksia *(R. Banksiae albaplena)*. The wonderful white rose of the South, originally from China. Hardy from South Carolina down with tremendous vigor, growing even to 60 feet. Evergreen foliage. Small, double, pure-white flowers in clusters. Very early: in winter in Florida, with azaleas in Georgia. It has a fine sweet-violet FRAGRANCE. (The Yellow Banksia is lovely, too, but without fragrance.)

Yellow and Yellow-Blends

Bloomfield Dainty (1924). Everbl. Semi-Cl. The large clusters of long, pointed, orange buds open to clear yellow, 2-inch, single blooms which are well set off by bright green foliage. Spurts of bloom occur all summer. The plant grows 6 to 8 feet and makes an excellent ground cover or ornament for a low fence. Slightly FRAGRANT.

Cl. **Break o' Day** (1944). CHT. Clusters of large, semi-double, orange-to-apricot (fading to shell-pink) blooms. Unusually vigorous plants, 15 feet the first year. Utterly handsome June display repeated in the fall on established plants, with some flowers in between.

Cl. **Goldilocks** (1951). CFl. Large, true-yellow clusters of 2-inch flowers in a spectacular late-May display; and always some flowers through the summer; a little color fading but neither quick nor complete. Foliage small, shining, and leathery, bright green, a good foil for the yellow flowers. Vigorous growth to 9 to 10 feet. Grows well in Florida, California, and the South and is hardy without protection to at least Philadelphia. One of the most dependable yellow, everblooming climbers.

Cl. **Peace** (1949). CHT. A winner of medals and a great favorite with those who like huge blooms. (Personally I find such size unappealing and there is little fragrance, but mine is definitely a minority opinion.) Deep-yellow, ovoid buds; double, high-centered, open 5- to 5½-inch flowers, lemon-edged pale- to deep-pink, depending on age of bloom. Very strong stems and fine, dark, glossy foliage. Vigorous plant to 11 feet, but seems to bloom better if trained horizontally.

Cl. **Shot Silk** (1931). CHT. An aristocrat among blends. Large, high-centered, semidouble, pale-cerise blooms with a golden glow and an orange center; blooms in clusters all summer long, opening, and holding, exquisite form; excellent for trellis or pillar or arch. Strong stems and large, dark, *glossy* leaves. Vigorous to 10 feet. One of the hardiest CHT's. (Much better than Cl. Talisman of similar coloring.) Very FRAGRANT.

Doubloons (1934). LC. Saffron-yellow, ovoid buds; double, 4-inch, cupped, peachy-yellow flowers in clusters on strong, 14-inch stems; grand rose to cut. Each flower of a possible 10 in a cluster opens and fades before the next, thus producing an early and a long display. (Much longer period of bloom than King Midas but color not so good, tends to buff rather than gold.) Large, glossy, resistant foliage and vigorous growth to 15 feet with effective bloom by second year. Extremely hardy. Charming in companionship of purple Clematis Jackmani, and nice over an arch. Slightly FRAGRANT.

Elegance (1937). LC. Double, 6- to 7-inch, deep- to pale-yellow blooms, white at edges in fading. Long, strong stems; large, dark, glossy, resistant foliage. Glorious in bud and most effective bloom. For those who like exhibition-type flowers with heavy petalage, this is it. (Too big for me.) Vigorous to 15 to 20 feet when established. If you grow it on a fence, allow 40 feet, not a rose for cramping! Very hardy. For many this is the favorite yellow climber.

Gloire de Dijon. CT. Buff-and-pink or "rich creamy-white, tinged amber and pale blush." Who indeed can describe this indescribably exquisite blend of hues? Dean Hole called it "the best climbing rose with which I am acquainted. . . . Its flowers are the earliest and the latest; it has symmetry, size, endurance, colour, fine tints . . . and perfume." Robust and tall to 15 to 20 feet, it is also *surprisingly* hardy and worth trying in colder regions. Wonderful tea FRAGRANCE.

Golden Climber (Mrs. Arthur Curtiss James) (1933). LC. Long, pointed buds; semidouble, 3½- to 5-inch, golden-yellow flowers of Hybrid-Tea size and shape, borne singly on 18- to 24-inch stems. Glossy, resistant foliage. Unsurpassed among yellow once-bloomers. Absolutely tops with me. Needs two to three years to become established, then only training required; must be grown horizontally for good flower production but can be taken up, even to 30 feet, with canes spread sidewise as it mounts. Almost never any spraying (maybe for a few aphids) or pruning required. Said to be "first *hardy* yellow climber of importance." (Golden Pyramid, LC, cadmium-yellow, also Brownell, is probably tallest of all yellow climbers; Golden Orange Climber, LC, has considerable orange and orange-red in the gold. I prefer Golden Climber to either.) Tea FRAGRANCE.

Gold Rush (1941). LC. Orange buds; large, high-centered, double (24 petals), yellow-gold flowers, which do lose color in fading. They are produced on the huge new shoots of the current season, a great advantage. Exceedingly handsome, large, shining leaves. Not reliably hardy, and this one does blackspot badly in some gardens. Perhaps it does not belong under Excellent Climbers, but its undoubted good looks seem to edge it in, and it *is* FRAGRANT.

High Noon (1946). CHT. Shining, yellow buds; 3- to 4-inch loosely-cupped, double (25- to 30-petaled), lemon-yellow flowers with red tints right through season. Nearly thornless stems. Leathery, glossy foliage. Bushy pillar rose to 8 feet. Best for West Coast and mild climates.

Indian Summer (1938). CHT. Pointed buds; large (5-inch), semidouble (20 to 30 petals), open flame, yellow, and orange buds fading to tan; color intensifies towards fall; scattered repeat bloom; long stems. Leathery, bronzy foliage which rarely blackspots. Tremendous vigor to 30 feet; grand for the south wall of a house. Strong FRAGRANCE.

King Midas (1941). LC. Long, pointed, red-flushed buds; semidouble, 4- to 5-inch, cupped blooms of deep golden-yellow in clusters of 4 to 6. Intermittent bloom for six weeks from May to June, continuing after many other climbers have stopped. Vigorous pillar grower to 8 to 10 feet (20 feet in California). Outstanding among early once-bloomers, establishes quickly, very hardy. Looks well with Veilchenblau or Violette. Slightly FRA-GRANT.

Maréchal Niel (1864). N. Long, pointed buds; large, double, pendant, golden-yellow blooms, very lasting and in great all-season profusion. Rich-green foliage. Vigorous climber to 12 to 15 feet. If you live in the South or on the Pacific Coast, you must have this beauty; it is not hardy as far north as Philadelphia. Strong tea FRA-GRANCE.

Mermaid (1918). HBc. Hardy in Philadelphia without pro-tection and in Ohio, though generally described as "tender." If winters only occasionally hit zero, you are safe in planting this one. In California, as at Carmel, of breath-taking beauty, also good in Florida. Large (5- to 6-inch) single, ivory-to-pale-yellow blooms with amber stamens. Profuse and constant bloom, in ones and twos, notable in autumn. Dark, lustrous foliage, disease-proof, almost evergreen. Vigorous climber to 30 feet, also excellent as a rambling shrub or trailer, a good way to grow it in colder regions. Where questionable, winter with a soil mound; if it dies back, it will start up again. Unparalleled! One outstanding quality: it will do well in shade or semishade (certainly not dense). Pleasing sweet-clover FRAGRANCE.

Mrs. Arthur Curtiss James (See Golden Climber.)

Mrs. Whitman Cross (1943). CHT. Long, pointed, espe-cially fine buds; large clusters of 4-inch, semidouble, open orange-and-apricot blooms with a pinkish sheen, sometimes rose stripe on reverse; long stems. Repeated

bursts of bloom. Glossy, soft foliage. Excellent upright
grower to 10 fcet. Very hardy, and blooms first season
after planting. Tea FRAGRANCE.

Orange Everglow (1942). LC. Copper-yellow, 3-inch flowers.
Repeats bloom in September, sometimes in between.
Glossy, almost evergreen foliage. Vigorous plants to 15
feet. A color to use with care in a garden having reds
and pinks. Very FRAGRANT.

Ruth Alexander (1937). LC. Especially suited to climate of
Pacific Northwest where it is very popular. Long,
pointed bud; yellow-orange-red flowers, which are large,
semidouble, high-centered. June-flowering. Glossy,
leathery foliage. Vigorous to 6 to 8 feet. Very FRA-
GRANT.

SINGLE CLIMBING ROSES

Since some of you, like me, probably dote on single flowers
—roses and otherwise—I list here some excellent singles
among the Climbing Roses.

Bloomfield Dainty. Evbl. Semi-Cl. Orange to yellow, recurrent, FRAGRANT.

Cherokee Rose *(R. laevigata)*. Red, pink, or white, June,
tender, FRAGRANT.

Cl. Dainty Bess. CHT. Wild-rose pink, recurrent.

Evangeline. R. Pink, June to July, FRAGRANT.

Mermaid. HBc. Yellow, constant, tender, FRAGRANT.

Schoener's Nutkana. HNut. Rose-pink, June, FRA-
GRANT.

Sunday Best. CHP. Red and white, spring, slightly FRA-
GRANT.

White Banksia. B. White, spring, tender, FRAGRANT.

Yellow Banksia. B. Yellow, spring, tender.

CLIMBERS FOR THE SOUTH

In the South where temperatures do not fall to zero, the Climbing Teas, Climbing Hybrid Teas, Climbing Floribundas, and other climbers of questionable hardiness may be freely selected. Where the dormant season is brief and warm weather quickly following induces plants to grow again, varieties that can make fairly constant growth are important. Also an adaptable understock is essential, such as *Rosa odorata* or Texas Wax, rather than *R. multiflora japonica* which is more universally used.

The everbloomers and once-bloomers of the North make tremendous growth in the South, and so should only be planted where rampancy is no deterrent. Such Large-flowering Climbers as City of York, Dr. W. Van Fleet, Mary Wallace, Mme. Gregoire Staechelin, Paul's Scarlet, and Silver Moon will usually do well, but since weather permits, why not select for more constant display? Noisettes, Climbing Giganteas, and Bourbons, as well as the Climbing Teas, Hybrid Teas, and Floribundas are all within your lucky realm. For ground covers, choose the spring-flowering Bracteas or a Cherokee. If you live in the Lower South, by all means study the catalogs of growers who can supply the tender and glorious varieties that are so particularly for you. Here are some suggestions:

Alister Stella Gray. N. Orange-centered yellow, recurrent, FRAGRANT.
Belle Portugaise. HG. Flesh-pink, spring only, but very profuse.
Cl. Devoniensis. CT. Pink-tinged white, recurrent.
Cl. Floribundas in general.
Cl. Hybrid Teas in general.
Cl. Louis Philippe. CC. Deep-red, recurrent.

Cl. Maman Cochet. CT. Medium-pink, recurrent.

Cl. Marie van Houtte. CT. Creamy, pink-tinged yellow, recurrent.

Cl. Perle des Jardins. CT. Golden-yellow, recurrent, FRAGRANT.

Cl. Snowbird. CT (sometimes labeled CHT). Lemon-tinted white, recurrent.

Cl. Souvenir de la Malmaison. CB. Light-pink, for spring, FRAGRANT (and choice).

Elie Beauvillain. CT. Two-toned pink and yellow, recurrent, very showy.

Gloire de Dijon. CT. Buff and pink, recurrent, FRAGRANT.

Lamarque. N. Lemon-centered white, intermittent over a long season, tremendous grower, great Southern favorite, FRAGRANT.

Maréchal Niel. N. Golden-yellow, recurrent, choice for Lower South.

Mermaid. HBc. Single yellow, really everblooming, FRAGRANT.

Reine Marie Henriette. CT. Cherry-red, repeats, FRAGRANT.

Rêve d'Or. N. Buff, recurrent, FRAGRANT.

Solfaterre. N. Lemon-yellow, repeats, considered one of easiest and finest of Noisettes, FRAGRANT.

White Banksia. B. Pure-white, great height or excellent ground cover for South, early spring only, violet FRAGRANCE.

Yellow Banksia. B. Yellow and without scent, otherwise same as the white form.

CLIMBERS FOR THE SOUTHWEST

In the region called the Southwest where there are areas of no frost, frost perhaps once in five years, or zero temperatures regularly, climbers must be selected according to the local prevailing conditions. The roses listed here have been particularly satisfactory in places where summer heat is high and zero temperatures are expected every winter.

In the Southwest, plenty of compost or humus in the planting hole is essential, at least half by volume, and the soil should be tested to determine the amount of sulphur to add to make it slightly acid. Extra phosphorus in the form of superphosphate is usually needed also.

Irrigation is essential. Chlorosis, indicated by yellowing or mottling of foliage and due to an extremely alkaline soil, can be corrected by applying agricultural sulphur, and Trace-Tone is reported as a helpful correction for soil in this area. Some climbers seem more prone to chlorosis than others. Climbing Crimson Glory is one, but still it is recommended as being the most continuous blooming of the Climbing Hybrid Teas, and Climbing Talisman also is likely to be affected.

It is important to leave adequate space between wall and plant. Most gardens are walled in this area, and the walls reflect considerable heat. Climbers under such conditions need a circulation of air around them. To hold them *near,* but not *next,* to a wall, use wall nails and hold the canes to them with long strips of raffia or nylon hose.

American Pillar. LC. Single, carmine-pink, late June-blooming, wonderful display.
Billy Boiler. CHT. Dazzling red.
Blaze. LC. Brilliant red, newer strains everblooming June through September, only slightly FRAGRANT.
Bloomfield Courage. R. Single, velvety-red, June-blooming, a favorite, growth unbelievable.

City of York. LC. Creamy-white, profuse once-bloomer, FRAGRANT.

Cl. Cécile Brunner. CFl. Pink-on-yellow, June-into-August bloom, excellent mass effect, beautiful little buds, slight tea FRAGRANCE.

Cl. Christopher Stone. CHT. Scarlet, one of finest, heady old-rose FRAGRANCE.

Cl. Crimson Glory. CHT. Ruby-velvet with almost-black shadings, as many as eight crops of bloom through season, very FRAGRANT.

Cl. Dame Edith Helen. CHT. Glowing pink, scanty bloom but recurrent, old-rose FRAGRANCE.

Cl. Etoile de Holland. CHT. Bright red, FRAGRANT.

Cl. Heart's Desire. CHT. Crimson, desirable but slow to start, very FRAGRANT.

Cl. McGredy's Ivory. CHT. Creamy-white, yellow base, FRAGRANT.

Cl. Mrs. Pierre S. duPont. CHT. Golden-yellow, profuse bloom, but a tendency to chlorosis, FRAGRANT.

Cl. Talisman. CHT. Golden-yellow and copper, better than bush type, very FRAGRANT.

Cl. Texas Centennial. CHT. Vermilion-red, excellent.

Dr. Huey. LC. Maroon, June-blooming, very showy.

Kitty Kininmonth. HG. Deep-pink, heavy June bloom, sparingly repeated, slight FRAGRANCE.

Mme. Grégoire Staechelin. LC. Delicate-pink, stained crimson, May-June-blooming, fine old favorite, slight FRAGRANCE.

Paul's Scarlet Climber. LC. Scarlet, profuse June-flowering, only slightly FRAGRANT.

Silver Moon. LC. Pure-white, June-blooming, slightly FRAGRANT.

Wind Chimes. HMs. Single, deep-pink flowers in "apple-blossom" clusters, colorful hips all winter, FRAGRANT.

CLIMBERS FOR THE NORTHWEST

In Seattle and Portland where a wonderful temperateness prevails, all the Climbing Hybrid Teas thrive. Climbing Ena Harkness from England is truly magnificent, and the Australian Countess of Stradbroke, notably remontant. I saw there, too, most attractive groupings with clematis, as the Blue Ramona with climbers Blaze and High Noon, and the pink species *Clematis montana rubens* which overlaps the white beauty of City of York in spring.

You will enjoy any of these climbers if you live in the Northwest.

Belle Portugaise. HG. Flesh-pink, spring only, but very profuse.

City of York. LC. Creamy-white, profuse once-bloomer, FRAGRANT.

Cl. Charlotte Armstrong. CHT. Tapering red buds, large brilliant cerise flowers, FRAGRANT.

Cl. Cherry. CHT. Brilliant carmine-pink flushed yellow, FRAGRANT.

Cl. Crimson Glory. CHT. Ruby-velvet with almost-black shadings, crops of bloom through season, very FRAGRANT.

Cl. Ena Harkness. CHT. Crimson-scarlet, very FRAGRANT.

Cl. Lady Forteviot. CHT. Golden-yellow to apricot, wonderfully FRAGRANT.

Cl. Lord Charlemont. CHT. Clear deep-crimson, dependably remontant, very FRAGRANT.

Cl. Mrs. A. R. Barraclough. CHT. Bright carmine-pink, yellow base, slightly FRAGRANT.

Cl. Mrs. Sam McGredy. CHT. Beautiful reddish-bronze

foliage, flaming copper-orange bloom. One of the most satisfactory, FRAGRANT.

Cl. Picture. CHT. Clear light-pink, everblooming, slightly FRAGRANT.

Cl. Pinkie. CFl. Rose-colored, profuse bloom, slightly FRAGRANT.

Cl. Poinsettia. CHT. Bright scarlet, slightly FRAGRANT.

Cl. Shot Silk. CHT. Pale-cerise, orange center, blooms all summer, very FRAGRANT.

Cl. Show Girl. CHT. Deep-pink, FRAGRANT.

Countess of Stradbroke. CHT. Dark crimson, FRAGRANT.

Guinée. CHT. Black-red with golden stamens, May-June and September-October bloom, very FRAGRANT.

High Noon. CHT. Lemon-yellow with red tints, blooms all season.

Mme. Grégoire Staechelin. LC. Delicate-pink with crimson stain, once-bloomer, most interesting seed pods, slight FRAGRANCE.

Renae. CFl. Pink, wild-rose FRAGRANCE.

Réveil Dijonnais. CHT. Clusters of large semidouble carmine-streaked yellow flowers, profuse in spring and remontant.

Ruth Alexander. LC. Yellow-orange-red, June-flowering, very FRAGRANT.

Zenith (Uetersen). Shrub. Rarely lovely, shining red, repeated bloom, very showy.

CLIMBERS FOR THE SAN FRANCISCO AREA

Where little sun, continued coolness, and fog are factors to be considered, choose climbers from this group, of which "Mrs. Sam" and Sungold are probably the best. In this temperate climate plants make tremendous growth, so be generous in your space allowance and give each plant 25 to 35 feet. I saw these doing handsomely even on small city plots where each was allowed the full length or width of the wall or fence which surrounded the garden.

Belle Portugaise. HG. Flesh-pink, spring only, but very profuse.

Cl. Etoile de Hollande. CHT. Bright red, FRAGRANT.

Cl. Lady Forteviot. CHT. Golden-yellow to apricot, very FRAGRANT.

Cl. McGredy's Ivory. CHT. Creamy-white, yellow base, FRAGRANT.

Cl. Mrs. Sam McGredy. CHT. Beautiful reddish-bronze foliage, flaming copper-orange bloom. Magnificent, wonderful FRAGRANCE.

Cl. Picture. CHT. Clear light-pink, everblooming, slightly FRAGRANT.

Cl. Pinkie. CFl. Rose-colored, profuse bloom, slightly FRAGRANT.

Cl. Red Talisman. CHT. Deep cerise-red, FRAGRANT.

Cl. Talisman. CHT. Golden-yellow and copper, FRAGRANT.

Cl. Yellow Talisman. CHT. Pale yellow, FRAGRANT.

Sungold. CHT. Bright golden-yellow pointed bud which does not fade in the open flower, big show then scattered blooming, glossy foliage, vigorous.

CLIMBERS FOR SOUTHERN CALIFORNIA

Where temperate and warm conditions prevail, and you can pick roses every day in the year, choose from these. Climbers here make unbelievable growth—50 feet is not too much for the spread of even one of them, and canes on old plants sometimes develop to 6 inches in diameter. I could hardly believe my eyes when I saw the extent and magnificence of climbers which even under ideal conditions in the East make only a neat, restricted, seasonal growth.

Belle Portugaise. HG. Flesh-pink, spring only, but very profuse.

Captain George C. Thomas, Jr. CHT. Single yellow, FRAGRANT.

Cl. Capistrano. CHT. Bright pink, free bloom, sweetbrier FRAGRANCE.

Cl. Christopher Stone. CHT. Scarlet, heady old-rose FRAGRANCE.

Cl. Dainty Bess. CHT. Single, wild-rose pink.

Cl. Heart's Desire. CHT. Crimson, very FRAGRANT.

Cl. Lady Forteviot. CHT. Golden-yellow to deep-apricot, very FRAGRANT.

Cl. Lorraine Lee. CHG. Golden apricot-pink, recurrent, FRAGRANT.

Cl. Mark Sullivan. CHT. Orange-gold-yellow, very FRAGRANT.

Cl. Mrs. Sam McGredy. CHT. Beautiful reddish-bronze foliage, flaming copper-orange bloom. Most satisfactory. FRAGRANT.

Cl. Peace. CHT. Lemon-edged pale- to deep-pink huge blooms; yellow buds.

Cl. San Fernando. CHT. Scarlet, profuse bloom, very FRAGRANT.

Cl. Shot Silk. CHT. Pale-cerise, orange center, blooms all summer, very FRAGRANT.

Cl. Texas Centennial. CHT. Well-formed, vermilion-red, with a spread of 50 feet in Los Angeles.

High Noon. CHT. Lemon-yellow with red tints, blooms all season.

Mermaid. HBc. Single yellow, very free-flowering, FRAGRANT.

Mme. Grégoire Staechelin. LC. Delicate-pink with crimson stain, once-bloomer, most interesting seed-pods, slight FRAGRANCE.

Sombreuil. CT. Flat, well-formed, creamy-white, very FRAGRANT.

Sungold. CHT. Bright golden-yellow pointed bud which does not fade in the open flower, big show then scattered blooming, glossy foliage, vigorous.

Ramblers and Trailers

FOR MANY OF US the old-fashioned Rambler Roses still
have great appeal. There are even those who "collect" them;
cheaper they say than antique-collecting and, of course, for
them more fun. Modern roses, Large-flowering Climbers,
and Hybrid Teas, to be sure, have greater individual beauty,
but for sheer power of profusion, Ramblers still hold their
own. Crimson Rambler, introduced in 1895, first made
Climbing Roses popular. Soon many hybrids were introduced. These were generally planted in the eastern part of
this country and have proved so enduring that it has been
said you can date an old house by its roses. (Students of later
architecture will probably do it by surviving plants of Paul's
Scarlet or Van Fleet.) Only two fairly-recent introductions
have been introduced in the Rambler class. The excellent
Chevy Chase appeared in 1939. Brownell's Rambler or
Brownell's Yellow Rambler—it is known both ways—appeared
in 1942.

Derived from *Rosa multiflora* and *R. Wichuraiana,* the
Ramblers bear dense clusters of rather small flowers, usually
in June or July, though some like Tausendschön start in

May. Individual flowers are, as I have said, not distinguished but the quantity of color is marvelously effective. Ramblers are usually once-bloomers only, setting their flower buds on wood developed the year before. In health, when not affected by mildew, the foliage is glossy.

A Rambler-type of rose has a well-defined habit of growth. The term Rambler is apt because the varieties in this group do ramble. A true Rambler produces long, thin, flexible canes that have little power to hold themselves upright and without support stay close to the ground. The more typical varieties have an indefinite kind of growth which elongates through the entire season when a really vigorous plant may produce 30-foot canes; 15 to 20 feet is average.

Most varieties send up a number of new canes each year from the base of the plant. They are also likely to produce long rapidly-growing canes from high up. Because the canes are so long and pliable, Ramblers are ideal for arbors, trellises, and fences, or to cover banks. They are less well adapted to pillars or posts because of their excessive vigor and, if the canes are cut to check growth, they invariably branch out and continue the elongation. Dorothy Perkins is an example of a true Rambler.

Ramblers have been dear to our hearts now for half a century. To enjoy them, give them the space they need. If crowded, or planted out of full sunshine, mildew is encouraged. In most places, they must be protected from mildew by frequent spraying or dusting with sulphur. Wait for an under-90 degree day. A preparation called Mildex is also excellent.

Ramblers need more pruning than most other climbers and more training too, since there are so many new canes each year to direct in the way they should go. (These matters are discussed in Chapter 12.)

If you have an oceanside garden and can offer protection

from wind through shrub and tree plantings, fences or walls, you will certainly enjoy the Ramblers. No mildew there, and a blooming in the brilliant sunshine and moist air to please you beyond all possible expectation. Perhaps as a hobby you too will collect Ramblers. There are some thirty of them (more probably in private collections) still to be had, mostly from growers specializing in old roses. The catalogs of Bobbink & Atkins, Hennessey, Kern, Kohankie, Tillotson offer a number. Torch is only available, I believe, from Bosley. (Addresses of growers are given on page 198 ff.)

THE RAMBLER ROSES

Pink and Pink-to-Red Blends

Dorothy Perkins (1901). R. A cross between *Rosa Wichuraiana* and a Hybrid Perpetual, Mme. Gabriel Luizet, this made history. It is *the* typical Rambler (as Crimson Rambler is *not*), still popular and rightly so. Huge clusters of small, double, clear, rose-pink flowers appear in July. Few roses give a greater effect in bloom, making even the battle with mildew worthwhile. This one is common, but so beautiful! With some FRAGRANCE.

Evangeline (1906). R. A darling, 2-inch, single pink that looks like a wild rose. Actually it is rosy-white with deep-pink veining and comes in long-stemmed clusters. There are few singles among the climbers, so I prize this one. Most growers have let this charmer fall by the wayside, yet it is one of the choicest of the Walsh introductions, a cross between *R. Wichuraiana* and Crimson Rambler. It usually grows only 12 to 15 feet, and has rather dark, leathery foliage, larger than the type. FRAGRANT, too.

Minnehaha (1905). R. This one with delicate pink rosettes has a winsome appeal. Flowers are very small and double, and the pink fades to white. The large clusters last well into July. Usually free from mildew and slightly FRAGRANT.

Nokomis (1918). R. Double, rose-pink flowers, larger than those of Dorothy Perkins, come in variable clusters of 5 to 30. A wonderful vigorous climber (rare now). Very FRAGRANT.

Roserie (1917). R. A Tausendschön sport. Large (3 3/4-inch), semidouble, deep-pink flowers with a white base. A real beauty with a grand spell of blooming in June. Large and leathery foliage. Only slightly FRAGRANT.

Seven Sisters or Grevillia Rose *(R. multiflora platyphylla).* (1817). A melody of lilac-rose, soft pink, and almost-white flowers, with "seven tints in the same cluster." The individual blooms are larger than those of *R. multiflora* and appear in pyramidal clusters in June. The plant is somewhat tender; can grow to 30 feet, but 8 to 10 feet is more usual.

South Orange Perfection (1899). R. Rosette-form, blush-pink flowers come in clusters that turn white. This one is very hardy, and also FRAGRANT.

Sweetheart (1901). R. Rose-pink buds open to very double, 2½-inch, white flowers that are richly FRAGRANT.

Tausendschön (Thousand Beauties) (1906). R. Always outstanding in any collection of roses. Large, double, cupped flowers, both rose-pink and white, in large clusters on strong stems. Very early flowering, with profuse May-into-June bloom. It could drop its petals more cleanly; Roserie, which is similar, does this better. Foliage is soft; the canes thornless, and only 8 to 10 feet. Roy Hennessey calls it Pastel Pillar, a nice name. Only slightly FRAGRANT.

Universal Favorite (1898). R. Large clusters of double, soft-pink flowers that are FRAGRANT.

Red

Bloomfield Courage (1925). R. "The calico-print rose." Tiny, single, very dark-red (almost black), velvety blooms with white centers and prominent yellow stamens appear in good-sized clusters amidst dark foliage. This is a nice early one—late-May and early-June blooming. If faded flowers are not removed, a mass of red hips will develop.

Bonfire (1928). R. This is the dazzling color of fire with small flowers in clusters of 20 to 25 from May into June.

Chevy Chase (1939). R. "Finest of the Ramblers," it suggests an improved Crimson Rambler with lovely, small, dark crimson, very double (60 to 70 petals) flowers, singly or in clusters of 10 to 20 on short stems. Profuse bloom comes May into June, and the color changes with age but not unpleasantly. The soft, smooth, small leaves are very different from those on Dorothy Perkins. It is practically mildew-proof.

Crimson Rambler (1895). R. Irregularly-double, crimson flowers in large, pyramidal clusters in July. Of historical interest only, being very mildew-prone. Chevy Chase and Excelsa are better reds.

Excelsa (Red Dorothy Perkins) (1909). R. Double, cupped brilliant rose- to light-crimson flowers in clusters in June and July. (But the rich-green, glossy foliage does mildew, except at the shore.) Marvelously effective but watch its companions: it will dim most other colors or quarrel with them. Especially keep red Ramblers from naturalizing near the wild orange daylily. This makes a horrible picture in the New England scene in July!

Hiawatha (1904). R. Small, single, brilliant, white-centered, crimson flowers with prominent golden anthers in large clusters in July. For garden background, this can be more spectacular than Paul's Scarlet; it is good on alternate pillars, with the semidouble, pink Christine Wright, LC, or with any white. (In 1931 Hiawatha Recurrent appeared, but I cannot find it today.)

Yellow and Yellow-to-Orange Blends

Aviateur Blériot (1910). R. Very double (34 petals), orange-yellow, fading to white. The profuse June bloom has a lovely magnolia FRAGRANCE.

Brownell Rambler (1942). R. Some flowers are borne singly; others appear in looser, more open clusters than those of Dorothy Perkins. Yellow, very double with recurved petals; blossoms not particularly distinguished but interesting for the true Rambler look in yellow. They open in June and have a slight FRAGRANCE.

Cherub (1923). R. Small, pointed, yellow-and-salmon-pink buds; semidouble flowers in huge, clear-pink clusters, May into June. This looks like the Sweetheart Rose, Cécile Brunner. Cherub is a darling, and aptly named. The foliage is small, wrinkled, glossy, and rich-green; the canes almost thornless. Very vigorous where it is hardy; unlikely to survive below zero. Wonderful for the Deep South.

Easlea's Golden Rambler. Misnamed, it belongs with the LC's.

Gardenia (1899). R. I never thought of this favorite of mine as a Rambler yet so it is by birth, but the semidouble flowers are larger, to 2 to 3 inches, and in small sprays on short, strong stems rather than in tight clusters. A lovely, lovely rose, with pointed yellow buds, creamy-white, yellow-centered flowers. The dark glossy foliage is very *resistant*. No trouble, this one.

Ghislaine de Féligonde (1916). R. Bright-yellow buds open to 1-inch, cream-colored flowers in clusters of 10 to 20. Profuse bloom in June; sometimes later flowers, too, on new shoots formed through the summer. A restrained grower to 8 to 10 feet; not dependably hardy, but one of the prettiest of the Ramblers.

Jersey Beauty (1899). R. Large, single, pale-yellow-to-white flowers appear in clusters in June and are FRAGRANT.

Phyllis Bide (1923). R. The small, semidouble, soft-yellow flowers are pink-tipped with nice "corsage-type" buds for wearing and arranging. They come in long, loose clusters in June. This is only fairly hardy, not safe below zero. Also old blooms stay too long, turning green, but the profusion of flowers to cut compensates for the necessity of a final shearing job. The plant grows to 6 feet.

Torch (1942). R. The June clusters of small, scarlet-orange, semidouble flowers have a white eye. The plant climbs only to 6 to 8 feet. Slightly FRAGRANT.

White

Evergreen Gem (1899). R. Buff bud opening to double, white, 2- to 3-inch flowers in clusters. Almost evergreen foliage. Climber or trailer. Sweetbrier FRAGRANCE.

Félicité de Perpétue (1827). Sempervirens Major sport. Fairly large, blush to pale-cream flowers in large clusters. A Rambler which is particularly good as a ground cover and will bloom some hanging *down* from the top of a bank. Almost evergreen, resents pruning. Wonderfully healthy and hardy.

Fraulein Octavia Hesse (1910). R. This is a cross of *R.*

Wichuraiana with the marvelous Kaiserin Auguste Viktoria (HT), and so there is *recurrent* bloom along with a vigorous habit. The small, double, yellowish-white flowers have darker yellow centers, and they are FRAGRANT.

Manda's Triumph (1899). R. Very double, pure-white flowers in clusters of 10 to 12 are a lovely sight in June.

Sanders' White Rambler (1912). R. Large clusters of rosette flowers, medium-sized and glistening white. Better than White Dorothy Perkins. Sweetly FRAGRANT.

White Dorothy (1908). R. Creamy-white sport of Dorothy Perkins. I wish it faded more attractively.

White Tausendschön (1913). R. Like Tausendschön with pure-white or pink-flaked, white flowers.

Purple

Amethyst (1911). R. Nearer "blue" than Veilchenblau with great clusters of small, very double blooms in marvelously rich purple tones in spring. Shiny, disease-resistant foliage and long arching branches to 12 feet.

Veilchenblau (Violet Blue) (1909). R. Small, semidouble, cupped, purple flowers fading to magenta. The huge clusters come on short stems in June. The plant is so strong it has been used as understock but fading spoils this for a garden plant. It is now of historic interest only. (Violette is better.) It is FRAGRANT.

Violette (1921). R. Practically alone among climbers for this violet color. The buds open maroon in large clusters of 1-inch, ruffly, semidouble blossoms. The plant is not at all inclined to mildew. Outstanding in the garden, especially with a clear yellow like Golden Climber or Golden Pyramid which pick up the golden emphasis of Violette's stamens; or to separate pink Ramblers on a long fence, as Dorothy Perkins or Minnehaha. Because of color alone, this should be more widely planted. It reminds me of the wild purple aster.

ROSES THAT TRAIL

Many of the Climbing Roses are equally good at trailing, especially the Ramblers, and also those others whose very derivation makes them prefer a horizontal way of life. Every rose has a *"natural* angle of incidence, an inherited constitutional relation to gravitation," as Mr. Brownell has so pertinently remarked, and it is hardly possible to make it thrive at more than 45 degrees beyond that norm. Therefore many of the Brownell hybrids, being closely related to the ground-hugging Wichuraiana, perform best if allowed to trail rather than climb. They will even bloom *some,* but not so well, when growing *down* from wall or fence, and that in some circumstances is a valuable characteristic. Generally, it is best to start them low and let them trail upwards a little.

When varieties flower best as trailers it seems to me they should be so classed. To label Creeping Everbloom, for instance, as a Large-flowered Climber is somewhat incongruous, unless climber simply means length of cane and not uprightness or tallness of growth. However, let us not be academic. The qualifying descriptions of each species or variety are after all our safest guide.

When we want low-growing roses to cover rough ground, scramble over boulders or cut-out, grow *down* from wall or terrace, or along the sides of a flight of steps, we have an excellent choice. For any such use there are truly beautiful plants—both species and hybrids. You can buy the species mostly from growers who handle "old" roses (names and addresses on page 198 ff.), but *R. Wichuraiana* is generally available, also Max Graf.

And, please, when you plant trailers on a bank, don't just hollow out the soil and shove the roots in. True, these are unusually enduring varieties, but a little care in planting is important even so. You don't want the roots uncovered by the first heavy rain, or the whole plant perhaps dislodged for lack of anchorage. So—cut into the slope so as to form a shelf and spread out the roots on a cone-shaped pile of good soil, as you do in planting any rose. Then after watering well and firming the earth, provide stability with well-placed stones around the planting area. Thus there will be no surprises of washed-out roses found at the bottom of a slope.

Here then are trailers that will delight you, most of the hybrids being Brownell introductions. They have beauty, hardiness, and adaptability. I hope there is a just-right place on your property for one or two of them—even an untoward spot which has till now struck you as liability rather than opportunity. The trailers are so charming, and so little trouble.

There are *climbers* with a special affinity for trailing, too, as: the yellow Bloomfield Dainty, Bobbink & Atkins' White Climber, Climbing Renae (CFl, everblooming and with wild-rose fragrance), the lavender-pink May Queen, and creamy-yellow Mermaid.

THE TRAILERS

Pink and Pink Blends

Apricot Glow (1936). LC. The very double, apricot-pink flowers open in large trusses on long stems in June. The leaves are glossy and the vigorous plants grow to 20 feet. There is an appropriate fruity FRAGRANCE.

Coral Creeper (1938). LC. Deep-red buds open to semi-double, 4-inch, coral- to light-pink flowers with 1 to 15 of

them on an upright stem—an excellent bloomer with
lengthy foliage and a vigorous grower. It is very pretty
on a bank with Carpet of Gold; also good, as I have seen
it, pegged down to be a "bedding plant." It is FRA-
GRANT.

Little Compton Creeper (1938). LC. Single, deep wild-
rose-pink flowers come in open clusters amidst glossy
dark foliage. Canes reach 15 feet and "grow naturally
10 to 15 degrees above the horizontal"—a beautiful
robust plant with masses of yellow-orange-red hips in
autumn.

Max Graf (1919). RHug. This is an old favorite, completely
reliable. Single, pink flowers with golden stamens open
in June amidst handsome rugosa foliage. Here is a
strong grower in sun or shade with a reach of 20 to 25
feet, an extremely hardy plant, and with *R. Wichuraiana*
long one of the most popular ground covers.

Pink Cherokee or Anemone Rose *(R. anemonoides)*. This
hybrid of *R. laevigata* and *R. odorata* is a beauty.
Tender, of course, and only for the South, with large,
single deep-rose-to-pink flowers that keep coming
through the summer and are FRAGRANT.

White

Cherokee Rose *(R. laevigata)*. This is Chinese and not a
native American rose but it has so long been naturalized
in the South—it is now the state flower of Georgia—that
it seems to belong to us. Where it thrives, it is a magnificent trailer or climber with evergreen foliage and
canes 15 feet or more in length, even to 50 feet in some
places in Florida, though not in the coastal areas of that
state. It is tender in the North and if it does survive, it
rarely blooms. The 3-inch, pure-white, single flowers

have fluffy golden stamens and are richly FRAGRANT, suggesting the perfume of gardenias. (There is also a Double White Cherokee, really a semidouble sport, which I do not think is now available from growers; the Pink and Red Cherokee are forms of *R. anemonoides.*)

Evergreen Gem (1899). R. See above under Ramblers.

Rosa Wichuraiana (Memorial Rose). Single, 1½- to 2-inch white flowers with golden stamens come in few-flowered pyramidal clusters profusely through July. The dense, half-evergreen foliage always looks well and the canes make roots wherever they are covered with earth. This one is marvelous for holding banks and it produces a fine crop of bright-red hips in the fall. (Here is the kind of handsome species to make us wonder why we bother with hybridizing!) And it is FRAGRANT.

White Banksia (Lady Banks Rose). In the South and in California, this grows prodigiously either as a trailer or climber, traveling 40 feet or more. Rather large, tight umbels of tiny flowers appear early in the season. There are single and double forms, only the former producing the round hips. And there is a sweet-violet FRA-GRANCE.

Yellow

Carpet of Gold (1939). LC. The double, yellow, 2- to 3-inch flowers first open in early June and continue through the month. The shiny, resistant foliage covers a handsome plant which is one of my great favorites. It grows along to 12 to 15 feet, and sometimes in four years to 20 feet. Looks especially nice with Frederick S. Peck (LC), which is deep-pink with a yellow center. Carpet of Gold is FRAGRANT.

Everblooming Yellow Creeper, No. 110 (1945). LC. The 4-inch, semidouble (18- to 20-petal) flowers are golden and lovely. If tied to a pillar, the plant will also bloom on the perpendicular. Either way it grows about 15 feet in four years and resembles Carpet of Gold, but this one *repeats,* an added attraction, and it has tea FRA-GRANCE.

Golden Glow (1937). LC. A beauty, with double 3½- to 5-inch high-centered, spectrum-yellow flowers in abundance in June and well into July. The foliage is dark, leathery, and glossy. Vigorous to 20 feet either up or trailing. The FRAGRANCE is of tea.

Magic Carpet (1942). LC. Large double flowers open in a wonderful medley of yellow and orange shades. The shiny, resistant foliage covers vigorous 15-foot plants which are lovely with Carpet of Gold.

Memorial Rose (See *R. Wichuraiana)*

Yellow Banksia. The same as White Banksia except for color and its lack of fragrance.

Red

Creeping Everbloom (1939). LC. The double (30 petals), 4-inch, translucent-red flowers of Hybrid-Tea form come in clusters. This is free-blooming with recurrent bloom well into fall and it is FRAGRANT.

Red Cherokee or Ramona. This sport of the tender *R. anemonoides* bears light-crimson flowers all through the summer. They fade to rose-pink and are lovely and FRAGRANT.

CHAPTER SIX

The Most Fragrant Climbers

FRAGRANCE FOR ME is the most valuable attribute of the rose, more important than color, and, of course, more desirable than size. Indeed, I never sniff a faintly-scented or a scentless rose without feeling disappointed, even frustrated. Such beauty without fragrance seems to me an error of nature, perfume being the proper heritage of the rose. I would spare inches off Climbing Peace or Break o' Day, and sacrifice recurrent bloom on Blaze if instead I could have a rich perfume.

By fragrance I do not mean the kind the nose can detect when buried in a blossom, but scent as pervasive, unmistakable, and enchanting as that of the wild honeysuckle which on late June evenings fills my house with its determined sweetness. The source is in the nearby woods and meadows, hardly visible even from the terrace, but of undeniable power. There are some Climbing Roses which proclaim their presence with as delectable a perfume if there are enough flowers open at one time and the plant is close by.

Scented Climbers

Some of the scented climbers are species roses like the violet-scented *Rosa Banksiae,* the Macartney Rose *(R. bracteata)* with its hint of lemon, and the southern Cherokee *(R. laevigata),* which has the breath of gardenias. The Musk Rose *(R. moschata)* and many of its hybrids, particularly some of the Pemberton Pillars, have a marvelous characteristic odor. The Sweetbrier *(D. Eglanteria)* carries fragrance in its leaves.

Modern climbers with the sweetest fragrance are those whose heritage draws most heavily on "that famous trinity," *Rosa centifolia,* the Cabbage Rose; *Rosa damascena,* the Damask Rose; and *Rosa gallica,* the French Rose. Thus certain of the Hybrid Perpetuals will bring the "true old-rose scent" to your garden, but not, alas, that "chill and soulless beauty," Frau Karl Druschki, which nevertheless is such a handsome adornment for a pillar.

Hybrid-Tea Climbers, particularly the reds, and then the pinks, are usually well endowed with the damask fragrance we all love. Indeed we might say that varieties like Climbing Crimson Glory and Climbing Etoile de Hollande are more richly laden than their bush counterparts. Probably they only seem so because a Climbing Hybrid Tea carries in its greater burden of simultaneous bloom many more sources of sweetness than a bush.

In the Hybrid Tea, Reichspräsident von Hindenburg—which should not only have its name changed but be reclassified since it really is a fine pillar rose to 8 feet—we are richly blessed and we must demand its return to growers' catalogs. Its enormous, dark-pink blooms of cabbage form insist upon your pleased attention. The scent is recognizable at a distance, and, when you become aware of such a delicious perfume in a garden, inevitably you search till you find the source. This is an outstandingly sweet variety. Many other Climbing Hybrid Teas are also fragrant though rarely so much so.

Among the modern Large-flowered Climbers, which are not Hybrid Teas or only slightly related to them, there is much less fragrance, and we understand why. The hybridist must first be concerned with survival qualities in his roses. If they are not winter-hardy, if they are so delicate they are a prey to every disease, a joy to every insect pest, then beauty and fragrance are practically wasted. Only in warm and sheltered gardens, tended by constant and anxious hands, will they survive to cast their fragrance on the breeze.

With so many of the practicalities accomplished, however, for Climbing Roses, including the quality of repeated bloom, I hope fragrance will now be a more serious concern of those who make our roses. As Louise Beebe Wilder suggested more than twenty years ago: "We should beg of the wizard hybridists a race of more fragrant climbers. Certainly it is not beyond their skill to grant us this boon, and how much it would add to the delight of lingering in arbours and pergolas, and to the sweetness of our rooms beyond the casements of which clamber Rose vines."

In the group of large-flowered climbing varieties of notable fragrance, and having every other valuable trait as well, is certainly the damask-scented Dr. J. H. Nicolas, which first appeared in 1940 and has so well stood the test of time. Month by month it produces great, rose-pink, double blooms in clusters of three or four, and it grows to a beautiful 8 feet on a trellis. The dark-red Thor, which is much taller, but blooms only in early summer, then, however, for a six-week span, is another Large-flowered Climber for all of you to plant who prize fragrant roses. A number of others are listed for your convenience at the end of this chapter, among them

Parade, which I never pass without pleasure in its damask sweetness.

Source of Fragrance

There are frequent, and often sharp, disagreements among rosarians as to the quality, or the strength, of the fragrance of their favorites. Perhaps we should always keep in mind that as the same rose may smell quite different at different times of day, so our powers of perception wax and wane. Furthermore, we are not all born with a keen sense of smell, nor do we all develop the ability to identify or to describe fragrances. Our tastes also differ, so we hear one enthusiast raving over "the marvelous strawberry scent" of a variety which another describes as having the disgusting smell of over-ripe bananas.

What then is the basis of the perfume of a rose? Certainly "that sweet odour which doth in it live" is not a simple or a constant element, and, of course, in many cases it does not "live." When there is fragrance, it is due to the presence of geraniol, a substance containing oil of lemon, oil of orange, and oil of bay leaves. These so-called "essential oils" are present in varying amounts, and they evaporate at different speeds. Indeed, an individual flower in different stages of development will emit a different perfume, all of which adds to the fascination of roses.

Of course heritage determines whether a rose is fragrant or not. No cultural practices—no feeding, watering, or training—can make a scentless rose fragrant, but if it has the characteristic, certain environmental conditions of light, temperature, and moisture will emphasize it. A rose wet with dew in the early morning or dripping with rain will have little fragrance. Once after a shower, I checked over a large rose garden having numerous varieties known to be highly perfumed, and there was not a scent among them. They all smelled, not sweet, but simply wet.

It is the warm, morning sunshine which causes the oxidation of the rose oils, that is to say they are "released" upon the air, and breathing them in, we identify them as fragrance. Early in the morning before the alchemy of the sun has operated, there will be little fragrance even in a Crimson Glory. As the heat of the sun increases, however, so will the fragrance—up to a point. If the sun is so hot that more oil is released than the cells of the petals can replace, then there will be little sweetness during the noonday hours. Partial shade after midday is therefore an asset. In the cool of the late afternoon, fragrance will again be noticeable. A damp location also seems to bring it out, or the warmth of a room, as you have doubtless noticed when you have arranged a bowl of roses whose fragrance you hadn't noticed particularly in the garden.

As Mrs. Wilder has observed, a still moist, somewhat warm atmosphere is most favorable to the production of fragrance in roses. Extreme heat and drought, or long cool days, reduce it. But before a storm "the sweet odours will increase." Furthermore, there are roses which "give off their perfume to the air with more facility than others; certain Roses seem to be more fragrant in the autumn than in the summer, having an almost piercing quality of sweetness as the season draws to a close. 'And indeed,' wrote Bacon, 'the Nouember Rose is the sweetest, having been less exhaled by the sun.' And does it not always seem that the last Rose, 'wresting June from out the snows,' is the sweetest of all the year?" I am not sure, however, whether this last rose is sweetest or simply more appreciated since it stands alone.

I must point out too that the double rose is more fragrant than the single, despite the very special attraction all single flowers have for me. Not only are there more sources of perfume in the greater number of petals in a double bloom, but with so much petal surface covered, "the oils volatilize more slowly, and the perfume therefore lasts longer."

Nature of Rose Fragrance

As we have remarked, the presence of fragrance depends on the heritage of a rose; so also does the nature or quality of the fragrance. Some rather elaborate and arbitrary (it seems to me), classifications of fragrance have been suggested.

I find but three categories practical—Damask or Old Rose, Tea, and Musk. "Spicy" roses like Climbing Crimson Glory (which smells much like the clove pink) usually are spicy-sweet, so too with those roses which are reminiscent of strawberries, like Maréchal Niel, or of lemons, like Climbing La France. These may hint of fruit, but it is only a tang to a scent which is basically damask. As for the "wild-rose fragrance" of Mermaid or City of York, have these not really a delicate tea scent? And Musk Roses have a perfume that is simply "musky."

There are also some individual rather than group fragrances, like the violet odor of the white *Rosa Banksiae* or the hyacinth-sweetness of Maiden's Blush, and other indefinable but appealing scents which simply testify to a complicated and composite ancestry "since fragrance too is hybrid." Depending on your own experiences and preferences, a modern rose may suggest to you anything from "apple pie to new-mown hay," but not to someone else. There are also roses of hardly pleasant odor, notably those closely related to *Rosa foetida*.

Damask or Old-Rose Scent

The favorite rose fragrance is probably the damask, also described as the true, old-fashioned, rose scent. I believe no climbing *species* has this, but it is possessed by those *hybrid* climbers whose inheritance draws richly on Cabbage, Damask, and French roses, like the climbing forms of Hybrid Teas, such as the old Climbing La France (1893) or Climbing Killarney (1908).

Today you can easily bring damask fragrance to your garden with climbing forms of Crimson Glory, Christopher Stone, the "Daily Mail" Scented Rose, Etoile de Hollande, Radiance and Red Radiance, and Mercedes Gallart, remembering always that the Climbing Hybrid Teas are *relatively* tender. Among the very fragrant Large-flowered Climbers —and these have much greater hardiness—are Bess Lovett, Climbing American Beauty, Reichspräsident von Hindenburg, Dr. J. H. Nicolas, Parade, Thor, and Zepherine Drouhin, all with the fine old-rose scent.

Many of the Hybrid Perpetuals are of rich damask scent, and the taller growers among these, as Georg Arends and Général Jacqueminot, may well be grown as low climbers. They have the advantage of being very hardy. Not being true climbers, they are discussed in the chapter which follows on Could-Be Climbers.

The Noisettes

Where they are hardy, the Noisettes with their many-flowered, summer-and-fall clusters of white, pink, red, and yellow flowers, are choice, fragrant climbing plants. Besides the handsome golden Maréchal Niel, there is the lovely lemon-yellow Solfaterre, double, and so sweetly scented it is well described as "tops in climbing roses for the South." And there are also the pure-white, lemon-scented Lamarque and the buff-yellow Rêve d'Or. The Noisettes, supposedly crosses of *Rosa chinensis* and *Rosa moschata,* are the delight of those who cherish "a strong tea fragrance with a hint of musk."

Tea Fragrance

The tea fragrance—not pleasing to all and also as variable as are the scents of individual teas—was so-called for its resemblance to the pungent odor of *fresh* tea leaves, not to that of dried leaves or the brewed beverage. The progenitors of the Tea Rose are the blush and yellow forms of *Rosa odorata*. Being tender, the Climbing Teas belong primarily to southern gardens to which, in addition to fragrance, they bring the advantage of profuse autumn flowering. Among choice climbers with tea scent are the creamy-white Climbing Devoniensis, also called the Magnolia Rose; pink Climbing Maman Cochet; the sometimes-hardy, white-amber-blush Gloire de Dijon; creamy-yellow Climbing Marie van Houtte; golden Climbing Perle des Jardins; and cherry-red Reine Marie Henriette. And you might add Climbing Golden Dawn, a Hybrid Tea but with strong *tea* fragrance.

If the fragrance of roses is as important to you as to me, choose climbers from the group which follows. Plant them close to house or garden seat, and let them develop as large a frame as possible so that they can produce a profusion of bloom at one time. It takes a lot of fragrant blossoms to perfume a breeze!

Where Climbing Hybrid Teas are hardy, you can emphasize these in your choice. In cold regions, the three Large-flowered Climbers would be safer. In any case, this list includes various types, and each is determinedly fragrant, not such that you must draw close and breathe deep to catch the scent.

MOST FRAGRANT CLIMBERS

Cl. American Beauty. LC. Deep rose-pink, June, damask fragrance.

Cl. Christopher Stone. CHT. Scarlet, recurrent, heady old-rose fragrance.

Cl. Radiance. CHT. Rose-pink, recurrent, damask fragrance. (Also Cl. Red Radiance.)

Cl. Souvenir de la Malmaison. CB. Nicely quartered, rose-centered cream, masses of spring bloom, damask fragrance.

Conrad Ferdinand Meyer. HRug. Silvery-pink clusters, intermittent, damask fragrance.

Dr. J. H. Nicolas. LC. Rose-pink clusters, recurrent, damask fragrance.

Fragrant Beauty. Shrub. Carmine, continuous, spicy fragrance.

Gloire de Dijon. CT. Buff and pink, early and then later bloom, strong tea fragrance.

May Queen. HW. Lilac-pink, tends to be recurrent, strong, sweet fragrance.

Mercedes Gallart. CHT. Deep-pink to crimson (best in autumn), recurrent, damask fragrance.

Mme. Alfred Carrière. N. Pinkish-white, intermittent, damask fragrance.

Reichspräsident von Hindenburg. HT (but tall to 8 to 10 feet). Dark-pink to carmine, recurrent, damask fragrance.

Thor. LC. Dark red, long spring bloom, rich damask fragrance.

Wind Chimes. HMs. Deep-pink, recurrent, musky sweetness.

Zephirine Drouhin. B. Unfading rose-red-on-white, somewhat recurrent, damask fragrance.

CHAPTER SEVEN

Could=Be Climbers
with Fragrance

IN THE NORTH, the lover of scented roses who wishes to plant climbers may, without investigation, feel his choice is rather limited. Above Philadelphia, many of the Climbing Hybrid Teas have doubtful survival value and Climbing Teas are really hazardous, also most Noisettes. And among the Large-flowered Climbers, there are not too many scented varieties, and those are hardly of overpowering fragrance. But there *are* some marvelously fragrant roses, not usually designated as climbers but which are all reasonably tall growing. If trained to low fences, supported by pillar or trellis, and pruned to height rather than width, their ardent growth will make them most satisfactory climbers. Furthermore, several lusty growers can be enjoyed on a small property which otherwise would not have space for 5- by 5-foot, or larger shrubs.

These shrubs have very special advantages besides their gift of fragrance: they are unusually hardy. When established, they require almost no care, certainly not spraying or winter protection or feeding, and very little pruning. Generally they are called Shrub Roses, but I think of many of them as the Could-Be Climbers. I heartily commend these to you for all their individual worth and also because they will extend your rose horizon so delightfully to many worthwhile types perhaps not yet familiar to you.

Furthermore, these Could-Be Climbers put on a colorful fall and winter show. Plant a long fence with Rugosas, Musks, and other "Shrub" types and you will have an autumn sight to behold, and enough berried branches, mostly red and orange, but also black, to decorate the whole Town Hall at Christmas, and, in addition, make your own hearth and doorways a mecca for the neighborhood.

Among the Could-Be's are both old-fashioned and new Shrub Roses. I cannot pretend to do them justice in this book which is primarily concerned with accepted climbers, but I cannot quite omit them either. The tall Shrub roses are so right for our purpose. And, as George D. Greene of St. Louis remarked, "If you stay with roses long enough, eventually you will find yourself planting the old roses." Who indeed can resist them, especially when they are fragrant?

Bourbon and China Roses (Rosa Borboniana and R. chinesis)

There is no agreement on the origin of the Bourbons, except that the fragrant *Rosa chinensis* is one parent. Compact and vigorous with purple-shaded, bright-green canes, they produce delicious, damask-scented flowers in clusters, large or small. There are two important climbers among them—the flesh-pink Climbing Souvenir de la Malmaison (1893), known as Queen of Beauty and Fragrance, and the rosy-red and white Zephirine Drouhin (1868). There are also at least four exquisite Could-Be's.

Coup d'Hebe, Hebe's Cup, (1840) needs little more than its charming name to recommend it to me. Actually it has far more. In growth, it is much like a Hybrid Perpetual, and since it reaches 6 feet, it makes a fine pillar or trellis plant. The glossy, almost-evergreen foliage handsomely sets off the large, waxen, delicately beautiful, pink flowers whose rich profusion scents the July air. Sometimes plants are also recurrent.

La Reine Victoria (1872) generally blooms longer, spring through fall, and has such beauty that old-rose enthusiasts sometimes say, "If I could have but one of the old-fashioned roses, La Reine would be my choice." The petals, "like thin shells," are of soft, rich lavender-pink, darker on the outside. Buds are like balls (not "balled," though). The cupped flowers are long-lasting on the plant and also when cut. Pliable canes, 5 to 7 feet long, make this adaptable to fence-growing. The damask fragrance is intense.

Birdie Blye (1904), a China, is wonderfully dependable. Great clusters of small, fat buds open to 2-inch, very double, deep-pink flowers with a lavender cast; each petal is curled precisely back. It is for all who like Hermosa, with blooms like those used in garlands on little girls' spring straw hats. Birdie Blye's flowers are a bit larger and of deeper color, and it is truly everblooming. The vigorous plants grow to 6 to 7 feet and are good for fence or low trellis. It is strongly FRA-GRANT.

Gruss an Teplitz (1911), classed as a Hybrid Tea or Hybrid China, bears great, wonderful clusters of double, dark-crimson, 2½-inch flowers. These appear constantly on the bushy, vigorous plants which grow to at least 6 feet. The foliage is dark, too. The necks of the flowers are a little weak, but this does not detract from looks or performance and there is the true damask fragrance. What a rose is this one to grow as a climber!

. *Upper left:* Climbing Souvenir de la Malmaison (1843), an espe-
·lly hardy Climbing Bourbon, pale-pink and fragrant. *(McFarland,*
·oto). 30. *Upper right:* Thor (1940), a Large-flowered climber;
·imson, with sweet damask fragrance. *(Courtesy, The Wayside Gar-*
·ns). 31. *Lower left:* Zepherine Drouhin (1868), a red-and-white
·ourbon, hardy and very fragrant. *(Roche, Photo).* 32. *Lower right:*
·loire de Dijon (1853), a century-old fragrant favorite in a white-
·ber-blush blend, often hardy. *(McFarland, Photo).*

33. Climbing American Beauty (1909), a deep rose-pink Large-flowered climber with wonderful fragrance. *(Courtesy, Tillotson)*

34. Red Moss Rose, ancient, fragrant, and distinctive. (*Roche, Photo*)

35. Coupe d'Hébé (1840), a blush-pink Hybrid Bourbon, fragrant and tall. *(Courtesy, Tillotson)*

36. La Reine Victoria (1872), a rosy-pink Hybrid Bourbon, tall with intense fragrance. *(Courtesy, Tillotson)*

37. Mme. Hardy (1832), a fine white Damask with the sweetness of attar of roses. *(Courtesy, Tillotson)*

38. Ferdinand Pichard (1921), a striped red-and-white Hybrid Perpetual with fine scent and good height. (*Courtesy, Tillotson*)

39. Georg Arends (1910), a Hybrid Perpetual with delicate pink-satin flowers of strong fragrance. *(Courtesy, Tillotson)*

Cabbage Roses (Rosa centifolia)

Cabbage or Provence Rose, Rose of a Hundred Leaves, Rose des Peintres (because the eighteenth-century Dutch masters so often portrayed it), of ancient and devious origin, brings to our gardens a lovely spring profusion of soft, pure-pink flowers and fragrance of sweet old-rose quality. You will probably order it as Rose des Peintres. It will grow to 5 feet as a bush and bloom best when pegged down so that many short stems will develop. Planted beside a low fence, it can be trained sidewise, and the long canes will then produce many flowering stems from the leaf buds. Keep in mind, however, that it is tremendously and treacherously thorny and has only the one period of bloom.

Prune the centifolias after they bloom, and in early spring only to remove very old wood or to shape the plants a little, if it is necessary. They bloom on the old wood, you know, so don't sacrifice flowers by removing this in spring.

Vierge de Cléry is a lovely, snowy Cabbage Rose, considered by many to be the best white in this classification. It grows to 5 feet, and has a ravishing damask scent.

Moss Roses (Rosa centifolia muscosa)

About 1700, *Rosa centifolia* produced a sport which became famous as the Moss Rose. Today there are many fine hybrids. All who love old roses favor the Mosses with their crested sepals enclosing highly-perfumed flowers. At least three are fine for fence-growing. The Crested Moss or Chapeau de Napoléon (1827) bears fresh, clear-pink blooms in spring, and grows to 5 feet. If you have memories of an old garden sweet with Moss roses, you will know this one.

The Moss Rose, Comtesse de Murinais (1843), grows a little taller, to 6 feet, and its velvety, pale-pink buds open to shining-white, wonderfully fragrant flowers.

Jeanne de Montfort (1851) has a long season of bloom in spring, and its very fragrant, many-petaled flowers are clear-pink in many clusters on 12-inch stems. The vigorous arching canes reach 6 to 7 feet. This is a fine one for a pillar or a low trellis. If it is planted beside your house, you can enjoy a near view of the great mossy buds and revel in the pervasive perfume of the open flowers.

"Delightful to the eye, delightful for its fragrance and most delightful for its associations," as Canon Henry Nicholson Ellacombe remarked long ago. Who would forego the Moss Rose?

Damask Roses (Rosa damascena)

Supposedly brought to France from Damascus by a Crusader, the Damask Rose is cherished particularly for its heavy, rich perfume which always proclaims its presence, sight unseen. It will undoubtedly be planted with *Rosa centifolia,* and also *R. alba,* which is probably one of its hybrids, in the Garden of Fragrance which is being planned for the blind at the Brooklyn Botanic Garden.

The wonderful sweetness of *Rosa Damascena* has been bequeathed to many of our favorite Hybrid Teas, but the species itself is also worth growing. It produces an excellent spring profusion—sometimes repeated—of large semidouble, dark-rose flowers, and plants grow to 6 feet. This is the rose most esteemed for rose water and a source of attar of roses, too.

Of the hybrids, Mme. Hardy (1832) is really choice. As full-petaled as a camellia, the large, double, pure-white flowers—on occasion, blush-tinted—have an incurved center and a tiny green eye. This loveliest of old-fashioned, June-bloom-ing roses with its emerald-green foliage grows to 6 feet, and its perfume is unrivaled. (Having said so much I feel the comments I now must make should appear in very small type, but the fact is, in some untoward seasons, and in some climates, buds on this one ball, and foliage mildews. Even so it is so attractive where it does succeed, that it is well worth a trial along a fence in your garden.)

Maiden's Blush, a Hybrid Alba, appears here with the Damasks because it is probably closely related, at least its enchanting fragrance would proclaim so. This has been compared to the scent of white hyacinths, and who is not enthralled by that! Maiden's Blush is a charmer, very pale-pink to cream-pink on the petal edges, fully-double, the blossoms well set off by grayish foliage. It is a vigorous grower to 8 feet, handsome against a wall. Little pruning except for training is required, and the occasional removal of old wood when flowering ends in July.

Sweetbriers (Rosa Eglanteria)

The English Eglantine or Sweetbrier is an ancient, strong-growing, Shrub rose with a profusion of 2-inch, single, soft-pink flowers but with scent in its foliage to call forth memories and make for it lifelong devotees. Not when the sun is upon them, as with the fragrance of rose flowers, but when they are wet with dew or still dripping from a shower, is the sweetness of the apple-scented leaves sent forth. In a *Book About Roses,* published in England in 1869, Dean S. Reynolds Hole, a famous English clergyman and the leading rosarian of his day, wrote of the Eglantine, "So may the Sweetbrier, with no flowers to speak of, remind many a gaudy neighbor that fine feathers do not constitute a perfect bird, and that men have other senses as well as that of sight, to please . . . the Eglantine to me, when I passed through 'The Sweet Garden,' as it is called, just after a soft May shower, had the sweetest scent of them all.''

This is a lovely plant to train espalier-fashion under an often-open window in your house. Canes will reach up 8 to 10 feet, and long before the flowers appear, you will enjoy weeks of perfume from the foliage. Furthermore, it is a plant that apparently lives forever.

Perhaps the hybrids will appeal to you, too, the old Penzance varieties with the charming names from Walter Scott's novels, as Meg Merrilies or Anne of Geierstein, but they are hard to locate today except in old gardens.

The variety Lady Penzance with single, fragrant, coppery, yellow-centered flowers is still to be had (although in black-spot-prone areas, the pink species is a better choice).

Then there is the striking, modern, red Refulgence, not a Penzance hybrid and happily lacking foetida blood. The 7-foot shrub makes a good climber. The blazing scarlet flowers are large and semidouble, and the foliage is excellently fragrant in the manner of the Sweetbriers.

Hybrid Musks (Rosa moschata)

I cannot think of the Musks without excitement. Among them are some of my "best favorites," especially the Hybrids called Pemberton Pillars, which are some of the finest *climbers* we have, even if they are persistently classed as Shrub Roses. Cornelia, Penelope, and Prosperity easily cover a 6-foot trellis or pillar, while the species itself will ride a fence with exuberance or cover an unsightly area with loveliness. The small, single, white flowers appear through a long spring season—*sometimes* intermittently till fall, when in certain climates another big crop may be produced on long shoots. Whether you plant in sun or shade, you need not be surprised if this ancient beauty goes beyond 30 feet. Attractive small red hips cover the canes in the fall.

Prune the Musk hybrids by the little-and-often system, removing the ends of the flowering stems all through the growing season. Occasionally cut off an old cane at the base in spring. Then you will reap a lovely, flowery reward.

And what a fine fragrance pervades the garden blessed by Musk Roses. The scent is, as Mrs. Wilder remarked, "refreshing and delicious" but "curiously unroselike." Still it is warm, sweet, and delectable. As Canon Ellacombe said: "The scent is unlike that of any other Rose but it is very pleasant and not overpowering; and the plant has the peculiarity that, like the Sweet Brier, but unlike other Roses, it gives out its scent of its own accord and unsought, so that if the window of a bedroom near where this rose is trained is left open, the scent will soon be perceived in the room."

There are *at least* five of the Hybrid Musks, known as Pemberton Pillars, for you to become acquainted with at your earliest convenience. The very fragrant Prosperity (1919), with its fine trusses of double white blooms, and the pink-budded, single, white Kathleen have already been praised and included among 75 Excellent Climbers. (Wind Chimes is there also.)

Cornelia (1925) bears large pyramidal clusters of small fawn-apricot flowers, terra-cotta in the bud. This is really everblooming from summer into autumn, when the plant is at its best, and the flowers are superb. Foliage is bronze and glossy, and the vigorous growth reaches 6 to 8 feet. How excellent is this one to espalier against a high fence or train over a pillar, and it is well adapted to rather shady locations.

Pax (1918) is another beautiful white, cream to ivory, the pointed buds and great, semidouble flowers with prominent golden stamens being borne in handsome clusters. This is probably the largest flowering of the Musks and the plant is vigorous too, to 6 feet. Really everblooming, the fine arching branches make this a most decorative trellis or fence rose. And such fragrance! (Pax is hard to find but Bobbink & Atkins and Hennessey carry this though they may not list it.)

Penelope (1924) glows from June to October and gets more and more beautiful as the season advances. The large semidouble flowers, salmon- to cream-pink, are set off by glossy foliage, and the handsome plant grows 6 to 8 feet tall. Of course, it is wonderfully fragrant.

Hybrid Perpetuals

Before we had Hybrid Tea Roses the June-blooming Perpetuals—some of which flower intermittently through the season—were *the* garden roses. And today they are still appealing and worthwhile. At Elizabeth Park, I saw some flourishing beds of them that had been planted fifty years ago. They were still strong and beautiful, and most of the varieties marvelously fragrant too, excepting only Frau Karl Druschki, which nonetheless was handsome growing over a tall fence. There are at least five Perpetuals *of rich scent* to grow as climbers, if you wish. Most of them are pliable enough to train sidewise on a fence, which is the best way to encourage rebloom on varieties capable of it, since buds are produced from short laterals. These are encouraged to pop out at every leaf bud when a long cane is stretched horizontally.

Ferdinand Pichard is an outstanding beauty with semidouble, striped, red-and-white flowers opening on short stems which rise from every leaf node, and they keep coming throughout the season. Grow this one sidewise along a fence. The arching canes will bloom well this way and the crisp-looking, fragrant blooms command admiring attention.

Georg Arends produces rather-full first June flowers; later ones are obviously semidouble. All are high-centered of light, pure-pink, and large to 4 inches across with every waxen petal nicely curled to give a slightly pointed effect. It is definitely remontant. The fragrance is rich and sweet, a glorious rose.

Général Jacqueminot, the famous Jack Rose, appeared in 1853 and is still valued. In 1865 Dean Hole had to say of it in his *Book About Roses:* "Général Jacqueminot, for so many summers THE Rose of our gardens, is still a glory and a grace, its petals, soft and smooth as velvet, glowing with vivid crimson, and its growth being free and healthful. I well remember the time when we welcomed this conquering hero, in his brilliant uniform, as being invincible."

This historic cluster rose blooms heavily in June, and then some in fall *if* old flowers are removed. There is no midsummer bloom. The color blues somewhat so that flowers of three distinctly different shades appear at one time, but this is not objectionable. The plant grows to 7 feet.

A purple rose can be a lovely thing, and so it is with Reine des Violettes which opens lavender-rose with a velvety violet center and ages to a rich purple. Large and very double, with cupped petals, it flowers freely in early summer and intermittently later. It will grow 7 to 8 feet tall and delight you with every fragrant bloom. The dull, smooth, green leaves are also fragrant so that in bloom or out, you have wonderful scent at a distance of at least 10 feet, typically old rose in the foliage, somewhat sweeter in the flower, and practically thornless.

And what a beauty is Roger Lambelin, a Hybrid Perpetual with an oddity that confers distinction. The rich red flowers are all edged, and occasionally striped, with white, and the petals recurved. These are lobed and dented, too, like those of a carnation. Grow this one as a 6- to 8-foot pillar or sidewise on a fence, where like the others, it will tend to bloom more freely. It is beautiful and also full of scent.

Two other possibilities among spectacular, everblooming —and fragrant—Perpetuals are the pink Arrillaga and white Everest, but these are not for wet sections, since too much moisture makes them ball.

Rugosa Hybrids (Rosa Rugosa)

It is characteristic of the very thorny Rugosas that they are iron-hardy and resist every pest and ailment with their tough, usually-wrinkled, and very handsome foliage. For the seashore, for very cold or very dry areas, for untoward growing conditions anywhere, try the Rugosas as your climbers. These first five are notably fragrant, and beautiful, too, their excellent characters not detracting from their very good looks.

The fruit of the single and semidouble Rugosas is not the least of their attractions. Orange or red, almost as effective as the blossoms, it is a wonderful extra dividend for Christmas decorations. Such brilliant autumn adornment is found on few other sorts.

On Conrad Ferdinand Meyer (1899) the immense, double, silver-pink flowers appear in clusters in June and July, and again in September. The handsome, large, leathery leaves cover 12- to 15-foot plants which look fine on trellis or pillar, and if two plants are grown 8 feet apart and the tops joined they will make a self-supporting arch. The wonderful Gloire de Dijon fragrance is present in this cross, which is probably one of the most remontant of all the Rugosas.

Dr. Eckener (1931) looks more like a Hybrid Tea than a Rugosa and is especially handsome. It will grow to 10 feet, and is better not planted near true pinks. The semidouble, rose-over-yellow flowers are exquisite and they recur the season through. This one is for pillar rather than fence-growing.

Sarah Van Fleet (1926) also bears Hybrid-Tea-type blooms,

large, semidouble, of clear light pink, and from June to October. "Nasturtium-rose fragrance," says one enthusiast. The fine erect bush covered with glossy leaves reaches 6 to 8 feet.

Schneezwerg (1912), translated, means Snow Dwarf which sounds better, but since the plant grows tall, we wonder whence the name. The pure-white, semidouble, flat flowers with prominent yellow stamens look like Japanese anemones and appear from June to October. The brilliant, waxed fruits, first orange then turning bright red, develop along with the white flowers. From June on, they give a lovely effect though in successive crops, the first ones not surviving. The plant grows to 7 feet and the fragrance, not so strong as in other varieties, is agreeable to some.

Nova Zembla (1907), a sport of Conrad Ferdinand Meyer, inherits all its excellence and blooms in June and sometimes again in September. The flowers are ivory-white with a tint of blush.

Then there is Agnes, a yellow Rugosa with many lovely qualities of beauty and scent. It is a tall grower to 7 feet, but I include it with certain reservations: It is sometimes the "aphids' joy and a blackspot spreader," the ever-present tendency of *Rosa foetida* descendants, which Agnes is, being only about twenty-five percent Rugosa.

Scotch Roses (Rosa spinosissima)

The ferny, spiny, Scotch roses with their arching, garlanded canes will grow even in sandy soil. They practically take care of themselves, except for some of the hybrids whose foetida inheritance again leads to blackspot. My selections are free of this. The species bears small pink- or yellow-tinted flowers, the buds red-tipped. Plants are listed as growing to 3 feet; actually they go to 6 or 7 feet.

Rosa spinosissima altaica, the true Altai Scotch Rose, is very vigorous. Studded with white flowers, it is a sparkling sight in May. On a long fence-planting some Scotch Roses are a good idea since their globular fruits are usually black, a pleasing contrast to the red and orange crops of most other species roses. The Spinosissimas are, of course, extremely fragrant. The variety *lutea* is also excellent, very yellow, fading to cream.

Two of the loveliest of the hybrids have German names. Frühlingsgold or Spring Gold (1937) blooms in May and June in one glorious flush along the arching branches and "no shrub is more beautiful" then. Flowers are enormous, especially when you consider their profusion, 4 to 5 inches across, semidouble, a brilliant yellow in effect though they fade to creamy-white; fragrant, though less so than the species. The plant grows to 7 feet.

Frühlingsmorgen, Spring Morning (1941), is a single beauty, pink in the bud, cherry-red in the bloom with soft-yellow petal edges and maroon stamens. Also alight in May and June, it blooms occasionally later too, (constantly, I am told, in California) and is a better producer of hips than Frühlingsgold. In this case, fat little crimson "apples," an inch across, hang on the branches.

The Scotch Roses are not well suited to pillars or trellises, but they bloom beautifully strung horizontally along a fence.

Some Modern Shrubs

Drawing on many strains, hybridizers today have produced some very handsome Shrub or Semiclimbing Roses, often of recurrent habit, which are excellent additions to the garden. Grow them wide and handsome, as bushes, if you wish, or flat and beautiful, horizontally along a fence, or as low pillars where descriptions indicate the possibility of flowering on upright canes. All those I suggest here are of notable fragrance.

Fragrant Beauty (1950), a Shrub, is all its name implies from ovoid bud to 5-inch, fully-double, cupped, crimson-rose flower, which looks rather like a heavy-substanced Red Radiance and appears from June through October. Necks are a little weak, but this hardly matters if blossoms nod down from pillar or trellis. The foliage is handsome and the plant grows to 8 feet, and quite quickly, but it must have full sun and do not coddle it with rich soil. The fragrance is strong and spicy. Plant near a door so you can often smell it.

Hon. Lady Lindsay (1939) is among the very best of the Shrub roses. Clusters of pointed buds open to enchanting peach-pink, beautifully-formed flowers. These appear from June through October. (It looks like a very firmly-petaled, deeper New Dawn, which is one of its parents.) The young leaves are dusky purple; they change to dark green. This one is absolutely disease-proof. Canes are pliable and extend to 6 feet. The tea fragrance is strong.

Oratam (1939) is a modern Hybrid Damask of rich glowing color. The large, double, copper-orange-pink flowers with yellow petal reverses, are lovely but in a color to be used with care. June-blooming and with rugose, leathery, yellow-green foliage, it grows 6 to 8 feet tall and makes a handsome pillar. The rich damask fragrance is a lovely attribute.

Schoener's Nutkana (1930), a Hybrid Nutkana, of course, bears choice single, 4-inch, deep-rose flowers over a long spring season. Then a great quantity of brilliant orange hips enlivens the plant in fall. Arching canes make this excellent Semiclimber fine for an 8-foot trellis. The fragrance is most pleasing.

The Shrub Roses will extend the range of your rose-interest beyond types commonly accepted as climbers, and also bring the nostalgic charm of old-fashioned favorites to your place. Even if it is small, you can have three or four of these, since so many of them accommodate themselves to narrow *trained* growth or to low fence-growing. And remember that each has been selected primarily for its sweet, spicy, or aromatic scent.

I am sure that in selecting these few shrubs to grow as climbers I have omitted many that are excellent, but the choice is almost unlimited. Here at least is a *reliable* selection which is based first on fragrance and tallness, to be sure, but likewise on beauty of bloom, quality of foliage, and resistance to ailments. I also made an effort to include a representation of types, as Cabbage, Damask, Musk, Rugosa, Sweetbrier, and Hybrid Perpetual, to guide those of you who find it pleasant and desirable to have different categories of roses —but all generally of easy culture. I hope you will select for your Could-Be's a few roses that are as yet unfamiliar to you.

CHAPTER   EIGHT

Places for Climbers

ON EVERY PROPERTY, in every garden, there are a number of suitable places for Climbing Roses. For best flowering and avoidance of disease, especially mildew, give them at least six hours of sun a day—morning sun is best and full sun is still better but not essential, as you know if you have also grown acceptable climbers at north and west exposures. Late afternoon shade is desirable, especially for those of darker hue, some of which tend to blue or bleach when hot, bright, summer sunshine is prolonged.

A well-drained site is also important. Standing water damages roots. Nor does a layer of stones placed below them overcome the hazards of poor drainage. Indeed it makes the situation worse by drawing excess water toward the rose and holding it there. Poorly-drained sites require more than a few stones to improve them; they require well-laid agricultural tile—which happily for me is beyond the scope of this book.

On the House (Photographs 40, 41, and 42)

The place everyone has for climbers is against the house. I grow them there, nailing the great canes right onto the clapboards. I hear it's a dreadful way to grow Climbing Roses! It injures the wood, damages the paint, makes the painters mad, precludes proper air circulation—and looks just dandy! Where climbers don't have to come down for winter protection, I think it's a fine system. The rose vines naturally embower the house in this way and it's easy to train them around windows, up and over doorways.

When the time comes to paint, my policy is simply to depart, and let the painters carry on by themselves. I can only imagine the richness of their language—not for the ears of innocent children, I am sure—when they take down Golden Climber or Blaze.

Yes, some damage is thus done to plants every third or fourth year. Furthermore the painters also "simply depart" when the job is done, not attempting to put the climbers back in position. So I do it, pruning as I must, salvaging all I can. Plants are then not at their best for one spring, but they get into stride again the next year and look perhaps the better for the careful cutting and new training received in maturity. It is true, very pleasing patterns of growth can be worked out, espalier-fashion, when climbers are fastened right to the house.

Covering areas of the house with trellis-work or treillage is certainly a better system. At Little Compton, Rhode Island, the famous hybridizers, Mr. and Mrs. Walter D. Brownell have done this, and for twenty years Purity, Apricot Glow, and the deep-rose, rambler-type Roserie have grown beautifully, spaced as they are over the front of their house. (Photograph 41.) And at Mt. Kisco, New York, Mrs. Mortimer

J. Fox, the herb and lily specialist, has covered her white-shingled home with treillage as a support for many vines.

Treillage should be held out about 6 inches from a house by an angle-arm or iron bracket, or you can insert blocks of wood to hold a trellis away from the house. This permits a free circulation of air, back and front, and, if mildew-prone climbers like the Ramblers are grown on a house, they are assured the full flow of air essential to their well-being. You can make good treillage with 1-inch round. Place it so as to carry your roses attractively up and then sidewise. At the Brownells' four strips go up and two across. Thus grown, plants produce a multitude of flowering stems at the level of the second-floor windows.

For this purpose choose vigorous climbers which will revel in lots of frontage. Among the possibilities are White Gold or Silver Moon; yellow Golden Climber or Elegance; pink American Pillar, New Dawn, or Mary Wallace; and red Thor or Dr. Huey. The narrow strips of soil between side-walk and house also offer excellent opportunity for planting climbers to grow espalier-fashion.

If you have a one-story porch or wing on your house, you can plant a grand and vigorous rose that will travel up and then have a field-day spreading out over the extension. At the Brownells', Golden Climber (long nourished by dish water, I am told), covers the roof of the kitchen ell with a carpet of pure gold.

On Nantucket Island all the small cottages are lovely with the bloom of climbers in July. Both pink and White Dorothy Perkins flourish there, and also American Pillar. This makes a roof look as if it were snowed under with apple blossoms.

Ramblers don't mildew at the seashore so you can decorate your cottage there to your heart's delight. Beside the "Dorothys," you might enjoy the red Excelsa or Chevy Chase, or the purple Violette. These will also be grand for scrambling over the places you probably know by this time will never become velvet lawn.

For plantings at the seashore, Mr. George E. Lippincott, who has grown climbers there for years, also suggests the fragrant amber-tinged-white Gloire de Dijon (which *covers* his garage), pink Climbing Cécile Brunner and Climbing Yellow Cécile Brunner, lemon-to-white Glenn Dale, white City of York, deep pink *R. setigera*, the Prairie Rose (for 12-foot entrance posts), Coral Pillar (10 feet in a summer), and the Brownell roses which are not done-in by tremendous exposure to the seashore sun.

On Garage, Pergola, or Over Garden Seat (Photographs 43 and 44)

Too often the garage has that afterthought look. You needed it and you built it, but how often you wish you could tie it down and make it belong. Climbing Roses will do just that for you, holding the building to the ground or relating it to the house, especially if the roses can travel a little, or a long, distance over a connecting breezeway or pergola.

The pergola has a special role these days, I feel, where so many small—and very comfortable but not very distinguished —houses are being built all alike. Erect a pergola at one side to make an outdoor room or extend it from the front of the garage to cover up the terrible utilitarian value of the doors, and I think you'll like the effect very much. I treated my garage to just such an extension and it looks very nice, indeed. But of course, I did it primarily to increase my vine acreage. I've *never* had enough room for the plants that climb.

40. A vigorous climber espaliered against the warm chimney-wall of a house. (*Gottscho-Schleisner, Photo*)

41. Purity, Apricot Glow, and Roserie on treillage at the Walter
C. Brownells' in Little Compton, Rhode Island. (*Genereux,*
Photo)

42. American Pillar covering the trellised rooftops of a cottage on the Island of Nantucket, Massachusetts. *(Philip Gendreau, Photo)*

43. Paul's Scarlet Climber on corner trellises of a garage. (*Roche, Photo*)

44. Blaze adorning a pergola with a garden seat. (Gottscho-Schleisner, Photo)

45. A well-trained climber over an informal entrance porch. *(McFarland, Photo)*

46. Blaze covering the trellis work of a formal portico. (*Gottscho-Schleisner, Photo*)

47. Miss Dorcas Brigham's long, rose-covered rustic arbor at Williamsburg, Massachusetts. *(Earl R. Herrick, Photo)*

48. Pink Dorothy Perkins Ramblers over an arbor in a formal garden. *(Genereux, Photo)*

49. Climbing American Beauty on a stone wall. (*McFarland, Photo*)

50. Climbing Roses over a board-and-wire enclosure. (*Gottscho-Schleisner, Photo*)

51. Blaze on a picket fence, enjoyable from a porch. *(McFarland, Photo)*

52. Pleasure for every passer-by when Climbing Roses spill over a fence. *(Gottscho-Schleisner, Photo)*

53. Climbing Roses on a stone-and-picket boundary (*Gottscho-Schleisner, Photo*)

54. Climbing Summer Snow on a post-and-rail fence. *(Gottscho-Schleisner, Photo)*

55. For an ideal garden background, Climbing Roses over a split-cedar fence. (*Richard Averill Smith, Photo*)

Over the Entrance (Photographs 45 and 46)

A Climbing Rose to frame the entrance is another charming possibility. You can either espalier a vigorous grower at one side and train it up and over, or you can plant a pair of pillar roses—not necessarily of the same variety—one on either side. You can let these travel up side trellises and fasten them to the existing portico. Or on a flat-front house, you can build a well-proportioned arch to frame the doorway.

Make the arch sturdy and of adequate size. Skimpy arches crowd the doorway. They don't welcome guests, rather give them the claustrophobic sense of entering a narrow tunnel. Furthermore, roses develop side shoots which extend inward as well as outward from the trellis, thus making the inside of a low, narrow arch a thorny hazard.

The peak of the arch should be 16 to 20 inches over the top of the door, and there should be 20 to 24 inches of space on each side between doorframe and trellis. On such an arch a Climbing Rose looks utterly beautiful. I think, for instance, of a gray-shingled house with white shutters and trim and a glorious sweep of Blaze trained—not rampant—over it.

But don't put a Climbing Rose in such a prominent place unless you have in mind to take some care of it. It will have to look attractive all the time—and if it does, you'll love it. For a turquoise-blue door, any of the pinks would be charming, such as Dr. J. H. Nicolas, Inspiration, Parade, or the sweet single Evangeline. Or you might prefer a yellow like Mermaid, if it is hardy, or Violette planted with a large white clematis like Henryi. Or how about the fluffy-petaled white Polaris? For a vermilion doorway, that would look well, too, or a yellow like King Midas, the stamens of the one or the petals of the other to bring out the yellow in the red. With a white door, you could use any rose, even a deep-toned one like Orange Everglow or a blend like the rose-over-yellow Dr. Eckener. And how about Climbing Crimson Glory or the red-and-white Roger Lambelin (which is labeled Hybrid Perpetual, but it will climb)?

Beside a green door you could plant the crimson-rose Fragrant Beauty and so intensify both the red and green; or you might like the cool effect of the buff-and-pink Gloire de Dijon, if you are not in too cold a region. Of course any color rose will look well with a green door.

Whatever you plant at the doorway, though, don't you think it should have a sweet perfume? In Chapters 6 and 7 you will find descriptions of the most fragrant roses that do or can climb.

And please, please, if your house is of red brick, keep red roses away from it. Recently I saw an utterly handsome specimen of the maroon Dr. Huey espaliered on a red-brick house. The result was an absolutely sick-making combination. The specimen was so flourishing, too. I kept being both attracted and repelled; the color combination was something I hope time will let me forget. That plant of Dr. Huey, now, on a white house would have been superb!

For an Arbor (Photographs 47 and 48)

A whole arbor for climbers is something pretty special. Even if nothing else is planted there, the roses make the long covered walk a garden in itself. In Miss Dorcas Brigham's garden at Williamsburg, Massachusetts, there is an arbor-garden of such marvelous proportions that I have had it carefully measured for the record.

The height is 7 feet; the length 170 feet. The upright posts are spaced at 12-foot distances. The width is 12 feet, and there is a 6-foot flagstone path running through the center and bordered by 3-foot beds of nepeta *under* the arbor. *Over* the arbor are spread great plants of Blaze, Hiawatha, *R. multiflora* and *R. multiflora cathayensis*, American Pillar, and Max Graf. Grapes grow in between the roses—Caco, Moore Early, Concord, Niagara, and Delaware—and also a plant of porcelain-berry *(Ampelopsis brevipedunculata)*.

Along the outside of the arbor there are long 3-foot-wide beds in which the roses have been planted, also a pleasant collection of daylilies and tree peonies, all bordered with white sweet alyssum. When the red, pink, and white Climbing Roses are in bloom in June and the grape leaves are new, and below there is the yellow, pink, and white symphony of perennials, this arbor is a picture you never forget. If *you* decide to have such an arbor, don't reduce the 7-foot height or the 12-foot width. These make a proper vista to frame handsomely with roses.

On Garden Fences and Walls (Photographs 49-54 and Portfolio 9 and 10)

There isn't a fence made that isn't a natural for Climbing Roses or bush roses grown as climbers, for many of the climbers and most of the big bush kinds bloom better when grown horizontally or in a fountain. Roses look charming on every type of white picket, of course; also on picket-and-stone combinations; post-and-rail; high or low snow fences; wire-and-nail and wire-and-board combinations; and, of course, on every type of wall.

If walls are high and of cement, stone, or brick, you can soon get roses over the top by flinging old tennis or fish nets over the walls. Canes easily catch in these and are supported in their upward climb. Or you can cover a high wall with a sort of trellis-work of 8-foot (or taller) bamboo lengths (set at 8-foot intervals), with heavy wires strung between at 2-foot distances. (One mail-order house has 12-foot bamboo fishing poles listed for 97 cents.) I've seen this bamboo business and it works very well. Where long wires cross, hold them firm with shorter twists of wire fastened to special masonry-nails. You can buy these in hardware stores. They come in various lengths, and the shanks are grooved.

Mrs. Harold C. Whitman has used these net and cane contrivances in her beautiful Bedford Village garden in New York. She has also most knowingly combined clematis vines with Climbing Roses. (The nets are particularly good for these two.) The white Silver Moon, purple Clematis Jackmani, and plants of blue delphinium near a bed of yellow-to-pink Peace roses made a beautiful harmony; also the pink Dr. W. Van Fleet and the pale blue Clematis Ramona, in the company of Boston Ivy. And I have liked Silver Moon with Clematis Duchess of Edinburgh, both white; and Clematis Henryi with American Pillar for late June into July.

On low walls, as 18-inch garden dividers, you can trim rose plants to a single cane and let them run—and flower—along the top. Little Compton Creeper or any of the trailers are so decorative this way. And they are attractive also grown at the *top* of a dry wall. Being trailers, they will tumble down and not pine for upright growing. *Rosa Wichuraiana* is lovely so. And, of course, on a gray stone wall Golden Glow is a magnificent sight.

But about fences. If you haven't any and want them for extensive rose-growing—and why wouldn't you?—let me tell you, there are all manner of ways to achieve fences. In this do-it-yourself age, you can obtain various kinds from the big mail-order houses which specialize in all manner of garden furnishings, many in the knock-down state, painted or unpainted, for you to erect and finish.

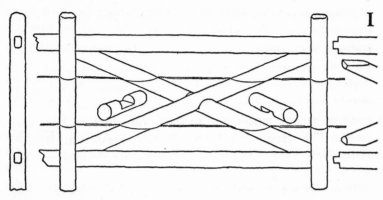

Natural cedar rose fence of poles about 4 inches in diameter. Horizontal rails mortised into posts. Center of
cross rails mortised as shown. All joints are nailed.
Galvanized wire ⅛ inch in diameter looped around
posts and cross-rail pieces.

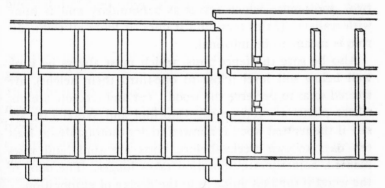

A checkered screen which can be used either as low
fence or tall enclosure. Openings can vary, depending
on size wood used. For 2x4's, first make 6-foot sections
of checkers 18 inches square off center. Sink mortised
4x4-inch posts ⅓ finished length in holes 6 feet 2 inches
apart. Insert section, add next post; nail 2x4 along top.

Lumber-yards are most accomodating also about cutting wood to your specification for fences, arches, pergolas, trellises, even garden seats; some suppliers like the Southern Pine Association (New Orleans, Louisiana) issue catalogs of designs. There are also Reader Services from which you can obtain, for nominal sums, all kinds of actual-sized plans for trellises, arches, fences, and so forth, on which to grow your roses. The Home Workshop Pattern Service at Bedford Hills, New York, has some most attractive designs and patterns.

However you plan to obtain the pleasant adjuncts to rose-culture, keep in mind that all elements should be sturdy. Poor fence materials sag very quickly, and a miserable weak garden arch is an offence to the eye. Most roses are powerful vines. They really lean on their supports. The only un-reliable fence I use is the 18-inch (36-inch height sawed in two), snow-fence which serves as a boundary and is hung with trailers. If this sags—and it does—it looks all right. Its role is meant to be informal.

Also be sure the fence-posts, which must always be sunk well below soil level (close to one-third their height), are treated so as to preserve the wood. Tar and creosote are out where plants are concerned. Cuprinol and Wood Life are safe if the treated wood is allowed to dry thoroughly—at least ten days to two weeks—before posts are sunk and roses planted. Sometimes evaporation takes longer. The odor of the wood is the best guide as to the degree of evaporation.

The most lasting posts are of redwood, hickory, or cedar, the cost depending to some extent upon shipping charges. Redwood would be the most economical and appropriate for the Far West, while hickory would be less costly and more at home in eastern, southern, and midwestern gardens. Also, I do think there is something to woods being appropriate to the locale.

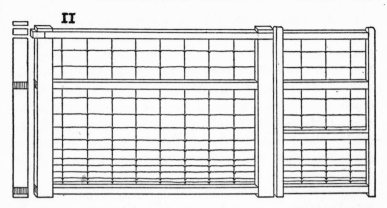

An easy and inexpensive wire fence on a well-proportioned wooden frame. Rails are 2 x 4-inch stock: bottom and second rails are 6 feet long, top rails longer, to cover tops of posts. Bottom rail 1 inch above ground, second rail ⅓ total height of fence from top.

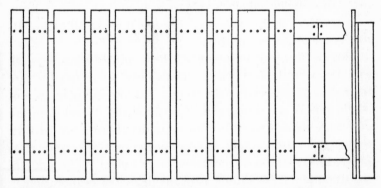

Plain board fence of any height, painted or left to gray. Planks may be random-width, equal-width, or wide and narrow alternating. Planks 4 inches higher than length of 4 x 4 posts above ground. Sink posts 7 feet 8 inches apart; nail two 1 x 6-inch stringers 8 feet long to post 6 inches off ground, and flush with top. Add planks, using galvanized nails.

There are some suggestions for fences in Drawing I and Drawing II. In Drawing II, details are given for making an unglamorous type (but who will know when it's rose-hung?) of wire on a wooden frame. If you want to enclose a large or small space inexpensively, this is the fence for you. In Drawing I are sketches of a fence used at Elizabeth Park, where Director Everett A. Piester grows roses to such magnificent perfection. I liked this sensible design, also the board-and-wire fence in process of being rose-covered in Photograph 50.

With certain cottage-type houses or grander homes in New England, or the South, as at Williamsburg, Virginia, the white picket-fence along the street, or enclosing a dooryard flower-garden, is suitable and attractive. Plant the climbers preferably on the property side where you can care for them properly. Their exuberant spring and summer bloom will delight all who pass.

Post-and-rail fences are excellent for country or suburban properties, and such a joy to all of us who want lots of climbers and lots of room for them. Low-growers of pillar type like Climbing Hybrid Teas, Climbing Floribundas, or many of the Large-flowered Climbers, or tall Shrubs should be planted at the posts. Trailers, Wichuraiana hybrids like Golden Climber, or any of the Hybrid Perpetuals can be planted between posts and tied right off to the first rail and then directed sidewise. Consult the various descriptive lists in this book for heights of your favorite climbers, or maybe select some Could-Be's or Ramblers.

Tall Garden Enclosures (Photograph 55)

If you want privacy for your garden or a shield for a service area, you might erect a tall fence of split cedar or grape stakes or a lattice fastened to square posts. You will

A lattice of many uses: try a pair at front corner of garage, or one on either side of doorway, with a third one across top. Side pieces are 1x2-inch stock; rest is ¼ x 1½-inch lattice. Horizontals are nailed to back to form square openings; cross pieces are then nailed with mitered joints. The spring in the material takes up unevenness.

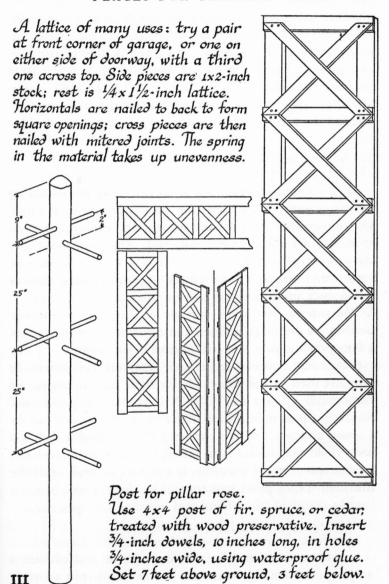

9"

2"

25"

25"

Post for pillar rose.
Use 4x4 post of fir, spruce, or cedar, treated with wood preservative. Insert ¾-inch dowels, 10 inches long, in holes ¾-inches wide, using waterproof glue. Set 7 feet above ground, 3 feet below.

III

then have a marvelous place to grow the big old-timers like Silver Moon, American Pillar, Mary Wallace, and Mermaid, if it's hardy in your climate, and Thor is fine, or the new Everblooming Brownell Pillars which laugh at 15 feet, if you give them four years to do it in. With them, of course, the whole area of lofty fence will be covered pretty steadily through the summer with roses.

On Trellises and Pillars (Photographs 56-59)

All the Climbing Teas and so-called pillar roses (that is, upright growers, if I understand this devious term), are nice for trellises, whether these are straight and form the sides of an arch or are fan- or fountain-shaped. The important thing about a trellis is that it stand next to a wall or be part of some other supported structure. A sadder sight than a trellis stuck up in open lawn or garden space I do not know. *So the rule for trellises is—not alone.* Excellent readymade trellises are available, painted and unpainted, but don't buy a flimsy one or your rose will outlive it ten to one.

Somewhere between trellis and pillar are two makeshift supports used by the Brownells for their Everbloomers. In Photograph 57 you see Pillar No. 73, the deep-rose one, covering a post-and-bamboo structure, which, placed beside a house in a series or at a property line would not look too bad. (I do not admire it in the open.) Also in the colored photograph 4, in the Portfolio, is a picture of what I call the Brownell Tepee pillar structure. The three, 8-foot bamboo lengths thrust in the ground and wired at the apex make a good support for lofty pillar-type growth.

I particularly like the T-shaped pillar which forms a kind of arch over a kitchen walk in Photograph 58; and, of course, proper pillars are excellent for a row of climbers in a formal garden. Drawing III is a modification of the excellent pillars used at Hartford. *But* beware of many pillars—or any—in an informal setting. They just aren't right for it. Incidentally, clematis and Climbing Rose plants are excellent grown on opposite sides of a pillar. The clematis climbs right through the framework of the rose. You can work out color schemes of simultaneous bloom or let later-flowering varieties of clematis continue the pageant begun by the early June roses. (See Chapter 9, Companions for Climbers.)

Over Arches (Photographs 1, 2, 4, and 60)

Garden arches are of many kinds from the wide wire-and-hollow-pipe affair familiar in old gardens and the rustic ones with seats to the more formal arch-and-gate type which graciously welcomes the guest and frames a vista. Whatever is chosen, it is important that the arch should be tall enough (even to 9 feet) and wide enough (usually to 6 feet), and that it should have a purpose. It should not stand bleak and unattended as a central lawn feature, a more frequent use than I could wish.

An arch should be placed so that, passing through it, you go from one definite place to another definite place. Don't let your affection for roses lead you to purposeless arching. Plant climbers against the house if there is no reason for you to have an arch. And remember if you do plant them beside an arch, you have to keep them in hand there. Photographs 1 and 2 are graphic illustrations of how roses should look on garden arches—also how they should not.

Along Steps, on Lampposts, Mailboxes, Wellheads (Photographs 61 and 62, and Portfolio 2 and 3)

The delightful trailers, Carpet of Gold, Magic Carpet, Little Compton Creeper, Max Graf, and the species *Rosa*

Wichuraiana and *R. laevigata* look charming on banks beside an easy flight of garden steps, or at the entrance to a property where steps have been cut from rock. One planting I much admire is on a 10-foot bank in a garden by the Sakonnet River in Rhode Island. At the top of the bank are Golden Glow, Copper Glow, and Frederick S. Peck, all Large-flowered Climbers; below are three trailers, the rose-pink Little Compton Creeper, Carpet of Gold, and Coral Creeper. They made a marvelous, glowing mass of color. Trailers are pretty, too, just covering a boulder, a decaying stump, or a rough area of ground. A place for trailers is a real asset on a property. Some trailers even do nicely going up a mailbox (Photograph 62).

A lamppost, a wellhead, a great dead tree trunk offer other possibilities for climbers. On dead trees they look so well that people who see them often wonder if they can't grow them, say, on their *live* maples, oaks, elms, or apples. This can be done on old trees where feeder roots are far away from the base, and if branches are lopped off to a height of say 25 feet, so climbers can get sun and air, they will do beautifully. Nearby evergreens, such as pine or holly, also welcome association with climbers.

And in rose gardens everywhere, climbers are important as specimens on pillars, as adornments for arches, on low dividing walls, or over tall backgrounds. Everywhere, everywhere—well, almost everywhere—Climbing Roses look lovely!

CHAPTER | NINE

Companions for Climbers

UNLESS YOU PLAN to grow only Climbing Roses on your place—which is unlikely—you will want to know of shrubs, vines, and garden flowers which, blooming at the same time, will create lovely pictures through color contrast or color harmony. A fine lawn has often been recommended as the most suitable setting for roses; doubtless it is a lovely foil, but, in my view, of but medium interest and, of course, monumentally difficult of attainment. I'd rather not count on "emerald sward" to set off *my* climbers. Furthermore, interesting companion plantings are always challenging to work out, and so rewarding when they are successful. Indeed the business of blooming combinations is a great game; climbers are pawns as useful in this arm-chair pastime as any other plants which afford a great mass of bloom over a long season. Even considering everything else that blooms in that almost too-rich period of late May through early June, Climbing Roses are still dominant.

Let's look now at some of the wonderful possibilities.

Since Philadelphia has a climate which represents a compromise between that of the extreme north and the south, blooming dates are given for that area. And, of course, they are relative, varying as they do with the weather from season to season.

EARLY POSSIBILITIES

The rose season begins in mid-May, or earlier, if the spring has been warm. A great many of the species roses, with mostly single flowers, bloom first. *Rosa Hugonis* is a charming example, perhaps too bushy to train *on* a fence, but its arching canes will drape *over* a low one beautifully. It has hardly finished when everything seems to burst at once: the first climbers show color, among them Bloomfield Courage, Mme. Alfred Carriere, Mme. Gregoire Staechelin, Tausendchön, Thor, Zepherine Drouhin, and last of the "earlies," but so powerfully not least, the ubiquitous Paul's Scarlet. The yellow *Rosa foetida* and its variants, *Rosa spinosissima* and its modern hybrids, Spring Gold and Spring Morning, and a great many of the bush roses, accompany these first climbers.

You could easily plan a garden of roses alone, but with most of us, I think the need is felt for plants of different leafage and form. A really overwhelming number of trees and shrubs also bloom at this time. Some, like the Catawbiense Hybrid Rhododendrons, the Mollis and Ghent Azaleas, Enkianthus, and other ericaceous things, would be gorgeous foils for many roses, but their vastly different soil requirements makes planting them as companions a feat most of us would rather not attempt. Easier to cope with are those trees and shrubs which will do well in the same more or less heavy soil as Climbing Roses. First, let's look at the possibilities of three trees. In a small garden just one of them would suffice, its rich blooming with an early climber a time of enchantment. (The catalog of Wayside Gardens at Mentor, Ohio, beautifully illustrates in color much of the material in this chapter.)

First of the Flowering Trees

Bechtel's Crab *(Malus ioensis plena)*. The large, double, pale-pink flowers and grayish-green leaves set this off from the other crab apples. Growth is at first upright, eventually to about 7 feet, then spreading to perhaps 12 feet. It is lovely with any of the pink climbers, especially the fragrant, cerise Zepherine Drouhin, and practically duplicates, in effect, Tausendschön.

Golden-Chain Tree *(Laburnum vossi)*. Upright to 9 feet, with long, hanging racemes of brilliant yellow to suggest the bloom of wisteria. This is a handsome sight paired with a clear yellow climber like Elegance or a blended yellow like Gloire de Dijon or the tinted Paul's Lemon Pillar.

Hawthorn *(Crataegus oxyacantha)*. The variety Paul's Scarlet (a shrub this time, not the climber of the same name) produces great masses of bright, rose-red, double flowers; variety *rosea* has single flowers of the same color, and both offer a fine extra dividend of fruit in fall, bright red and abundant. These trees form a great mound of branches, the lower ones easily sweeping the ground, so allow plenty of room. In time the spread could be 15 feet across. Both are lovely with white roses, in particular, City of York or Prosperity, also with *clear,* not salmon, pinks. The crimson-stained, pale-pink Mme. Gregoire Staechelin is a good associate.

First Shrub Companions

Here the possibilities are almost overwhelming. But what loveliness lies in well-selected shrubs with climbers! Actually the problem is not to overdo or crowd. *One* picture is better than three confusions.

Deutzia. The varieties *gracilis, parviflora,* and the hybrid of the two, *lemoinei,* all three make well-rounded shrubs under 6 feet. The tiny, pure-white flowers come in small clusters, but there are multitudes of them. *Gracilis* is particularly good (if you can get it true to name), for hiding the often bare base of a vigorous, woody climber like Silver Moon, and all are lovely as fillers in bouquets of roses.

Honeysuckle Bush. *Lonicera korolkowi* and *tatarica* are especially good. The first provides a striking color combination all its own: light gray-green leaves, quantities of rose flowers, and, in midsummer, bright vermilion berries. Any of the early climbers, pink like Kitty Kininmonth or white like Glenn Dale look well with it. *Tatarica* comes in many varieties, from deep rose to pure white, and bears masses of red berries in early summer, soon devoured by birds. It is more compact than *korolkowi,* but each will reach 7 to 8 feet. (Neither is fragrant, alas, as you would expect of shrubs so named.)

Neillia sinensis. This is a shrub once easier to find, but still available; it is a lovely thing both for growing with roses, and cutting for arrangements with them. A suckering plant to 6 feet, its arching branches bear small clusters of coral-pink bells, like a misplaced spray of *Heuchera rosamundi,* set off by deep red stems, and small birchlike, bronze-green leaves. With a pillar of Pink Cloud, a tint lighter, it would be exquisite.

56. Golden Doubloons on a trellis beside a brown-shingled house.
(*Roche, Photo*)

57. A Brownell Everblooming Pillar Rose on a post-and-bamboo trellis arrangement. *(Genereux, Photo)*

58. Climbing Lady Ashtown for a back-door pillar-crossbar.
(Roche, Photo)

59. Deep-pink Climbing Parade on an attractive pillar. (*Gottscho-Schleisner, Photo*)

60. Climbing Roses on particularly well-designed garden arches which frame a long vista. (*Richard Averill Smith, Photo*)

61. Single, pink, trailing Max Graf beside a flight of garden steps. *(Gottscho-Schleisner, Photo)*

62. Coral Creeper for a mailbox. (*Genereux, Photo*)

63. Climbing Roses as background accents in a rose garden.
(Courtesy, Jackson & Perkins)

Potentilla fruticosa. In its improved forms, this is a good, low, mounded plant, especially useful near the base of climbers, on the sunny side. Its buttercup-like flowers first open in mid-May, then continue all summer. It might well be planted with Climbing Goldilocks, or Mermaid, or a white climber with an open bloom showing its golden center, such as City of York. It would be splendid, too, with the plum-colored rambler, Violette, which begins to bloom in early June.

Spiraea vanhouttei, sometimes called Bridalwreath, surely needs no description. Its cascades of snow have much to do with making the world "white with May." It can be counted on to ameliorate the very redness of a rose like Paul's Scarlet and has almost too often been required to do so. It looks well with *any* climber so do choose a less usual companion. It is a great shrub growing to 7 feet or more and hangs over a low fence most gracefully.

Lilac *(Syringa microphylla and persica).* The more popular hybrids of the Common Lilac are on the wane by mid-May. These two less well-known species are small shrubs, under 6 feet, and widely bushy. Each has small leaves and small flower clusters in great profusion, *microphylla* pale lavender-pink, *persica* pale lavender, and each is fragrant. They are lovely with pale-pink, rose-pink, or the so-called purple roses, such as Violette or Reine des Violettes.

Tree Peonies. The modern American hybrids of *Paeonia lutea* begin in mid-May, and might be used for a really unusual combination against a background of fence-trained Climbing Roses. Perhaps this might even be too much of a good thing! All peonies have very handsome, lasting foliage, usually gray-green with coppery new growth, and the colors are so varied that you really

must see them in a nursery to select *the* one. The pale
yellow varieties, most easily obtainable, are lovely with
any Climbing Rose, white, yellow, or a blend like
Orange Everglow.

Japanese Snowball *(Viburnum tomentosum sterile)*. This is
the handsomest of snowballs, with horizontal branching,
bronze-green, pleated leaves, and small tight balls of
sterile florets. Its use is suggested here principally for
an unusual and enchanting effect based on the pretty
phenomenon that long before the florets turn white, they
are a beautiful pale green. A rose such as Birdie Blye, a
lavender-shaded deep pink, often difficult to blend with
other roses, would look superb against such a background—but it is a matter of timing!

Weigela. In all their rosiness, the weigelas begin to bloom in
mid-May, too. They are very hardy, and superior
varieties like the cherry Bristol Ruby might be used to
good effect near white climbing roses like City of York,
but by all means keep them away from Paul's Scarlet or
Blaze!

MIDSEASON HARMONIES

By the first of June, the great majority of the bush roses
are in bloom, and the midseason climbers have begun. Of
course, the early climbers, particularly those with double
flowers like Mme. Alfred Carriere or Thor, are still very
much in attendance. Silver Moon might be regarded as the
herald of the midseason group, which includes Max Graf,
Mary Wallace, Violette, Dr. W. Van Fleet and New Dawn,
American Pillar, Jacotte, and all the everblooming climbers
like Blaze, Parade, and Inspiration. These have all burst
forth by the middle of June at the latest. With them flower
an even greater number of woody plants than began in May.

Two are very large shrubs which to my mind are more effective trimmed to one or two trunks and grown as trees.

Trees for Backdrops

Russian Olive *(Elaegnus angustifolia.)* This is one of these. When full grown to 10 feet, its effect is not unlike that of a gray weeping willow, although branches hang *out* rather than *down*. Amid the whitened leaves in late May appear countless yellow stars, very apparent when you look up into the tree (though not from a distance). These have a very strong perfume, not at all cloying, as have the ligustrums which begin a few days later, and are so unpleasant to some people. *Elaeagnus* is a most handsome backdrop for any Climbing Rose, just as gray is to any other color.

Japanese Snowbell *(Styrax japonica)*. Here is another plant that can be either shrub or tree, depending upon its youthful training. By the first of June, its horizontal branches are strung with countless little white bells, very like our native Silver Bell, but in greater profusion. They have a very pleasant fragrance, too. This snowbell offers interesting horizontal contrast of form to any upright Climbing Rose.

Companionable Midseason Shrubs

Of the midseason shrubs, these are some of the very best.

Fountain Buddleia *(Buddleia alternifolia)*. Sometimes called Garland Flower, this hardy kind of butterfly bush does not die back over winter, but blooms on last year's drooping branches. The flowers are minute, and in small clusters, but these are strung in great profusion the length of each slender stem. It is both garland *and* fountain! And it is splendid near any of the pink climbers—as Dr. J. H. Nicolas or Dainty Bess—and would provide the fragrance that is lacking in a variety like American Pillar. There is no *pink* in the lavender of this flower.

Beauty-bush *(Kolkwitzia amabilis).* Here is a great favorite with those who know it. Before the end of May, its tiny, pale-pink flowers set amid new coppery leaves are borne in such quantity that branches are hidden. The color effect is similar to that of abelia which blooms much later, but this is far more showy. Good with any pink climber that has some yellow in it: Inspiration, Dream Girl, or the Shrub Rose, Hon. Lady Lindsay.

Mockorange *(Philadelphus coronarius).* This old favorite grows to 9 feet everywhere. Sweetly perfuming the evening air, it is in full bloom before the end of May. Since it is pure-white, it will look well with any climber, but might be best used with a beauty of such slight scent as New Dawn or Dr. Van Fleet. Its hybrids, the Lemoine varieties, begin to bloom a week later, and all are small shrubs, seldom over 6 feet, but also having flowers of the most exquisite fragrance. If you can find them, with reasonable assurance that they are true to name, the following are worth the search: Avalanche, Belle Etoile, Boule d'Argent, Mont Blanc, and Innocence.

Firethorn. *Pyracanthe coccinea* and its hardier more popular variety, *lalandi,* are included here not particularly for their blooming, although the clusters of small, pearlike, white flowers are modestly attractive against the new evergreen growth. Rather grow this for the possible fall combination of the intense orange of its tightly-bunched clusters of berries with the autumn-flowering of either a white Climbing Rose like Mme. Alfred Carriere, or a yellow, Mermaid or Bloomfield Dainty.

LATE ASSOCIATIONS

From mid-June to early July is late-climber season, Rambler-time. The small-flowers-in-huge-cluster-form of growth, that typifies Ramblers, makes their flowering very welcome. They take over the burgeoning of the everblooming climbers, while these are resting a bit and developing new buds. Chevy Chase, Minnehaha, Dorothy Perkins, Hiawatha, Excelsa, Evangeline—all belong here.

The Later Shrubs

Only one late-season shrub comes to mind as a companion for Ramblers and that can be really dramatic: Hydrangea macrophylla, the greenhouse hydrangea, a multicolored shrub that was doubtless originally a gift-plant of Easter or Mother's Day, set out for the summer! Its great heads come in every imaginable pastel from rich blue to white to deep rose. Although much has been written of the effect of alum and lime on the color, the entire gamut can appear on one plant, which might even be growing right next to one uniformly pink! With Climbing Roses, the stronger colors are better, although any blue hydrangea would go well with the warm tones of the Ramblers. Hydrangeas begin to show color by mid-June, and are at their peak during most of July. (Remember, August is the *only* month for pruning them.)

Before the glory of the Ramblers passes, the everblooming climbers have color again, and this appears more or less brilliantly until frost. Now there are a few summer-flowering shrubs to harmonize with these. All have a very long period of bloom, beginning in July and lasting into September.

Butterfly Bush *(Buddleia davidi).* There are many colorful varieties, the newer ones a great improvement over the old-fashioned tall lavender. Colors are rich and pure, with long racemes of florets all in bloom at once; plants are seldom over 6 feet—just right for planting in back of Climbing Roses spread out along a 3-foot fence. Purple Prince, an intense purple, its orange eye invisible at a distance, looks well with almost any rose, even the yellow blends, but not with a scarlet like Blaze, or a crimson, like Climbing Etoile de Hollande. The variety Fortune, a light lavender, is charming with true pinks and rose-pinks, and with soft, not bright, yellows. I think of Pink Cloud, Fragrant Beauty, and Bloomfield Dainty, offhand. Buddleias White Profusion and White Cloud, practically identical, seldom grow beyond 4 feet, and produce their short white racemes lavishly. They are particularly useful when associated with the un- sociable and queenly bright-red climbers. (Buddleias come in lavender-pinks and magenta also, but these colors don't mix well with most roses.)

Blue Mist *(Caryopteris).* This is a perfectly lovely little shrub, bearing long wands of clustered flowers that just miss being pure-blue through their touch of lavender. They flower about the first of August, and are effective well into September. This is considered a die-back shrub, like Buddleia, and even if some branches survive your winters, shear them back, since the plant blooms better on all new growth. Caryopteris needs full sun, and in it will develop a mound 30 inches high and 3 feet across. It blends beautifully with all those dark reds, such as Climbing Crimson Glory and Skyrocket, which Buddleia had best be kept away from. In fact, Caryop- teris will enhance almost any rose color. The only type I can think of, and that does not blend well with any-

thing, is an extreme red-and-yellow bicolor, such as
Climbing Talisman, a combination rare among climbers,
anyway. A new form of Caryopteris is now available,
only a shade deeper than Blue Mist, but of upright
habit; it is just as valuable.

Crape-Myrtle *(Lagerstroemia indica).* This darling of the
South is hardy farther north than is generally supposed.
There are a number of large specimens which survive
winters in the Philadelphia area, with little or no protection, and farther north it should also be tried more,
though as a die-back shrub. The various pinks and
watermelon-reds are the loveliest, and best with Climbing Roses. When established, a Crape-myrtle will be a
mass of color from late July into September, and it can
easily be trained to tree-form in regions where there is
no danger of serious winter-injury. So grown, it can be
depended upon to provide color near an "everblooming" climber that refuses to bud during summer
drought, for dryness has little effect on the Crape-myrtle.
The pinks are best near pale-pink climbers, like New
Dawn, but never near salmon-pinks; the "reds," which
are really deep brilliant rose, might be used with white
climbers, like Mme. Alfred Carriere, or also with very-
pale true-pinks like Climbing Radiance. Since this
shrub and its varieties repeat the rose colors themselves,
instead of complementing them, it must be used with
discretion. One magnificent Crape-myrtle, with one
superb climber, would be a September spectacle indeed.

Gordonia *(Franklinia alatamaha).* As shrub or small tree,
this is hardy at least to southern New York State, and a
real aristocrat. In cold regions, it has a better chance of
surviving winters when in shrub-form. The pure white
camellia-like single flowers, 3 inches across, begin to
open in early August and continue till frost; by that

time the large, handsome, leaves have turned a magnificent scarlet. Set it near Mermaid for these two,
single-flowered beauties are charming together, and
Franklinia's fragrance is also superb.

European Mountain Ash *(Sorbus aucuparia)*. This small
tree, grown just for its fruit, can be the August-Septem-
ber highlight of a northern garden, when it is laden
with large clusters of brilliant orange berries. These
also are perfect with yellow roses like Climbing Goldilocks, Bloomfield Dainty, or Mermaid, and in the Great
Lakes area, where this round-headed little tree is very
popular, the Brownell Everblooming Pillars would
surely make handsome companions.

SEASONAL PERENNIAL FRIENDS

In small gardens, Climbing Roses are more likely to be
grown not alone on far-flung boundary fences, but intimately,
as part of a flower border, or arising out of an interesting
undergrowth. Most of the hardy plants discussed here as
possible rose companions are doubtless quite familiar to you,
so I thought what might be helpful would be this correlation
of their blooming times. Then you can see at a glance which
will bloom with your once-blooming Large-flowered
Climbers, for instance. (Again the calendar is approximately
for Philadelphia.)

Early Favorites

Iris. To complement your early climbers select colors among
Early-Midseason and Midseason iris varieties which
bloom the last two weeks of May. Late-Midseason and
Late iris hold forth in the first part of June, together

with the stately Siberians, and a few varieties may be depended upon to provide a mass of color as late as June fifteenth. The countless lovely blues are the best for general use, as they harmonize with almost any Climbing Rose. (You *can* use too many colors in a garden!) A good blue sequence might be: Shining Waters, Fair Sky, and Princess Beatrice—all fragrant too!

Peonies. The new "herbaceous hybrids," in the most gorgeous colors, are at their height about mid-May, just as the early climbers begin. Their reds are of spectrum strength, to be used with discretion, but all the lovely salmon-pinks can be planted liberally. Early varieties of the Chinese peony, the more familiar kind, flower a little later, during the last week of May. Many lovely singles and semidoubles, so effective for landscaping, and in combination with Iris, open the season. Among them Festiva Maxima and Mons. Jules Elie. Midseason varieties like Felix Crouse and Philippe Rivoire begin in early June, and late varieties, which include some of the finest doubles, (Enchanteresse and Sarah Bernhardt), by June 10, in time to harmonize with midseason climbers! (These "seasons" are relative, of course, for each plant group. Thus Midseason iris does not bloom at the same time as Midseason hemerocallis, say.)

Daylily or hemerocallis. The old-fashioned lemon daylily, *H. flava,* makes a nice start in mid-May. Pale yellow and fragrant, it is sweet with any climber but a crimson. So too the variety, Winsome, which remains open at night, when its pale yellowness has the effect of white. It blooms from mid-May past the middle of June. Early-Midseason daylilies like Patricia and Serenade bloom in June. Midseason varieties are for July, like Hyperion, which is outstanding; Late-Midseason, July and August, like Lemon Luster and Sunny West; Late, August into

September, like Autumn Prince and Sonata, which usually continue until frost.

Delphinium. Form and color makes this almost indispensable in the June border. Easiest to grow are the sky-blue *D. belladonna,* with its *many* loose spires reaching 4 feet, and the deep-blue *D. bellamosum.* These bloom all through June, and again during midsummer and September, if faded stalks are cut off and the plants well watered. (A mulch of coal-ashes—rare in these oil-burning days—is your surest protection against the slugs and wireworms that love delphiniums even more than you do!)

For Midsummer

Now flower some hardy plants which are useful, handsome, and carefree.

Thalictrum glaucum, with graceful gray-blue-green foliage and pale yellow fluffs of flowers at 4 feet, harmonizes beautifully with most climbers.

Clematis recta gives much the same blue-green foliage effect, but during July and part of August, flowers of foamy, fragrant white, almost exactly like *Clematis paniculata* in both flower and odor, but on a wide 3-foot bush: a fine companion to that *lonely* climber, Blaze!

Lilium regale. This *one* lily which can be planted and forgotten must not be passed over. Tall (to 30 inches) and white with rosy reverse and very fine leaves, it can scent a garden most powerfully during July. What could be more beautiful than the combination of regal lilies and Climbing Roses? (You could not manage this too well with the bush Hybrid Teas!) *Delphinium belladonna* will accommodate you with a second blooming at just the right time, to make the picture perfect with a pink climber like Inspiration or a yellow like Climbing Goldilocks.

End of Season

Late summer provides more good associates, and almost all of them are blues!

Mist-flower *(Eupatorium coelestinum)*. This can be a pernicious weed, until you learn its habits. The green shoots do not put in an appearance until very late in May, sometimes at a good distance from where you remembered it last year. You can control it if in mid-June, when all the shoots are up, you simply pull out the ones that are annoying other plants. No more greenery will follow; from then on, the plant concentrates on developing a 2-foot height and many buds. It is charming near rose and pink climbers, also nice, I find, with Climbing Goldilocks.

Aster frikarti. This makes a fine rounded bush alight with large lavender daisies, through August and into September.

New England Aster *(Novae Angliae)*. Early September welcomes the first of the tall asters. There are not many of these, but the few there are, are very good. They multiply slowly, so mercifully do not need yearly division, and their stems have sufficient strength to stand upright without staking. Consider Violetta, a 2-foot mound of purple; Blue Plume, 3 to 4 feet and deep purple-blue; Barr's Pink, 4 feet, pink, very well branched; Harrington's Pink, 3 feet, salmon-pink.

New York Aster (Novi Belgii) is another story: most hybrids belong in this group, and they have in common rapid underground growth requiring yearly division, and a weak habit. Though some will reach 5 feet, they sprawl unsupported. For this very reason, they are ideal grown with fence-trained Climbing Roses. As the shoots reach upwards in July, head them in among the branches of the climber. Tall varieties will pass right on through! I am afraid I would stoop to any means to possess these marvelous asters, yet not stake them! Like many roses the asters bloom more profusely when horizontal. Among the best are Beechwood Challenger, 3 feet, bright crimson; Eventide, 3 feet, violet-blue; Plenty, 4½ feet, light lavender-blue; Gay Border Supreme, 5 feet, rich violet; Mt. Everest, 4 feet, white. These will escort the climbers to the end of summer, when the last frost is likely to find asters the only survivors.

Salvia azurea grandiflora, (also sold as *Salvia pitcheri*). Here is more blue and it is luscious. Native to Colorado, the form *grandiflora* is superior to the species: its flowers are a bit larger, pure brilliant blue, and it will not flop so helplessly as will the type. When not in bloom, it can be distinguished by the mealy whiteness of its leaves and stems. Like the other blue flowers, this one harmonizes beautifully with any of the rose colors. Great Azure Sage begins in late August, and continues until frost. Its blue clashes somewhat with the lavender-blues of the asters, but not with pure purple. You might give it the same supporting fence treatment as the tall asters, for it reaches 4 feet. It is simply breathtaking with rose-red and pink climbers.

Only one or two of these perennials need occasional spraying. Mildew and insects can bother both delphinium and New York asters in certain weather, but then, they'll bother the climbers, too. If you think it serious enough, you can dust or spray your hardy plants and your roses simultaneously with the same solution!

VINE ASSOCIATES

On first thought, you might say that vines have no business in the neighborhood of climbing roses, that, in fact, they are hardly necessary. This is indeed true of the vast majority. Wisteria, however, which blooms at the same time as the early climbers is lovely with them, if they are of powerful nature. On one pergola, it harmonizes with Silver Moon. "I let the two fight it out," the owner says, and that's what they have done successfully now for twenty years!

Three vines occur to me that are really suitable with Climbing Roses. They would certainly not harm them by strangling, and they have possibilities for enhancing the beauty of the roses.

Heavenly Blue Morning Glory. This first is an annual, and an old favorite. Offhand, I cannot think of one color among roses which the pure blue of this flower would not complement. If started early in plant-bands or pots, two or three plants set at the base of a Rambler after the July pruning would quickly grow up among the young canes, studding them with blue from August on. With the everblooming climbers, well-soaked seeds can be sown near the base about the first of May. The Climbing Rose's first bloom will be solo, but in August and September, when there is seldom the prodigality of the May or June display, morning glories will bolster the effect. After frost has finished them, the dried stems can be snipped out with little difficulty.

Porcelain-berry vine *(Ampelopsis brevipedunculata)*. The second vine is perhaps for growing *between* climbers, but not among them. It is worthwhile if only for its magnificent late summer and fall display of blue and purple berries. A truly unique plant. Even among shrubs, there is nothing that produces such unusual fall color. The vine climbs and clings by tendrils; it can be depended upon to grow 10 feet in one season if it is severely cut back each February. (Miss Brigham grows it, as I told you, on her long arbor.) The flowers are inconspicuous, but the fruit, by the first of August, begins to show color in a wonderful way. Some of the berries are destined to be purple, but these are first pale green, then lavender; the rest are to be ultramarine blue, but they start as the same pale green, then pass through aquamarine and turquoise, finally turning the deep color. All of these variations are present at one time in great quantity. This is a vine for growing *only* with the everblooming climbers, and for the sake of September, and then at a respectable distance, so that perhaps strung along a lengthy fence, the masses of roses and vine just meet.

Clematis. This is *the* vine for pairing off with Climbing Roses, but not the lovely May-flowering *C. montana rubens,* nor the September-blooming *C. paniculata* which scents the evening air of that season as pervasively as does honeysuckle in June. Both are too vigorous, and the first must bloom on its last year's growth, so will not stand annual disentangling. But the large-flowered clematis of midsummer, in all its wealth of varieties, goes with Climbing Roses. The clematis color-range might be said to begin with deep red, passing up through all the rosy colors to white, then down again through lavenders to strong violets and deep purples. If you can, name a rose one of these will not enhance! While it is possible to use those varieties which must not be pruned in early spring, but which will bloom on their growth of the previous year, I think the effect might prove more trouble than it was worth. The varieties which must be cut back severely to 18 inches in March are the best to use with Climbing Roses. There are many from which to choose.

Clematis Varieties

Crimson Star, bright garnet-red

Mme. Edouard Andre, purplish-crimson

Ville de Lyon, carmine

These reds are best with white climbers; Mme. Alfred Carriere, City of York, Silver Moon.

Comtesse de Bouchard, rose

Duchess of Albany, bright-pink

Nice with whites, or very pale pinks; especially fine with Dr. W. Van Fleet, which blooms only once.

Henryi, White

With pale pinks, pale yellows, try with Blaze or even white for an odd contrast of form.

Ascotiensis, medium violet-blue

Mrs. Cholmondeley, lavender-blue

Prince Hendrik, lavender-blue

Ramona, pale-blue

This is the most useful group. It will complement beautifully pink, rose, rose-red, crimson, yellow, and orange climbers, but not the strong salmon-pinks or scarlets.

Jackmani, violet-purple

Gypsy Queen, true purple

These *will* set off the salmon-pinks, also pink-to-rose, yellow-to-orange, and many blends of yellow and rose, but not good with rose-red, scarlet, or crimson.

Ten feet is about as much as clematis will grow. Most of them have begun to bloom by the first of June, some even in May, if planted in full sun (with the base of the vine shaded). They will bloom through all of June and July, and again in September. Considering the way Ramblers grow, it does not seem wise to attempt planting the large-flowered clematis with them: these roses, once mature, grow about the same length each year, and in July, must usually have about half their bulk removed. But clematis may very well be grown with the once-blooming climbers.

Clematis climbs with its leaves, the long petioles (stalks) of which twist with a tendril-action around anything narrow. If planted next a post, wires must be fastened the entire length, to provide something for the vine to grapple onto; set near a Climbing Rose, clematis has its support grown to order and happily clambers among the canes. After winter has withered it, and it is possible to find stray flowers on clematis vines even in December, snip the stems here and there, disentangling the snarl bit by bit. This is the only price you pay for a rather dramatic and unusual display all summer, and I hope you will think it is worth while.

CHAPTER   TEN

Planting Is No Problem

In the planting and care of your Climbing Roses, you can be as plain or fancy as you like. Training and tying them is important—and a pleasure I think—but in extremely cold areas, winter protection is rather a chore. Otherwise climbers thrive and are truly beautiful and rewarding with very little attention. Even the Climbing Hybrid-Tea type needs much less dusting or spraying than bush counterparts, while the Brownell Everblooming Pillars with their "built-in" health and below-zero endurance perform practically on their own, once they are established on your place.

If you want flowers for exhibition or are frantic about having the "biggest and best" in your neighborhood, you can be "fancy," prepare immensely-deep planting holes with special-formula soil, and you can go in for an intensive program of fertilizing, perhaps give regular foliar feedings. You can keep a sprayer or duster very busy too. But if mass of bloom—with plently of enjoyment—is your aim, follow me the *plain* way.

When to Plant

In most areas, you can set out Climbing Roses in either spring or fall, *according to your own convenience*. If you live where prolonged zero, or below, temperatures prevail, and there isn't likely to be a continuous insulating layer of snow, better choose spring, and as early as the condition of the soil permits. Plants will then have a chance at some root production before they are tempted by warm weather to work at vegetative growth and flowering.

It is sometimes pointed out that the cold-storage plants supplied in spring suffer from being out of the ground all winter. Perhaps when winter storage was less well managed, this was a valid objection. Today the big suppliers dig plants with such care and store them under such ideal conditions, that the buyer in spring from a reliable firm of rose specialists need not beware.

Actually the hazard of spring planting is weather. Early spring is so unreliable. It's always too cold or too wet—or we're too busy! Plants never seem to arrive at just the right time, and then there's the problem of heeling-in, perhaps, which I consider a monumental bother. And in some years a sudden hot spring is disastrous to plants which have not been in the ground long enough to establish their roots. However, I have some nice climbers which were planted in July in an emergency year. They have grown beautifully with no special care that first summer beyond plenty of attention to watering.

Where winter weather is only rarely of below-zero cold— and it suits your convenience—by all means, I'd say, plant in fall. October is a grand month for the job, and the weather is almost always favorable.

Fall planting means a fine long rooting period since growth

continues even in very cold weather. Temperatures a few inches below the surface do not prohibit rooting, and through most winters there are long, fairly-warm weeks when a lot is accomplished which we don't see. Of course, an unusual cold spell for your particular area or poor summer conditions, resulting in a supply of not well-matured plants, may mean winter losses or considerable die-back. You can be skeptical either way, but don't be. Both fall and spring are generally satisfactory planting times.

Only in areas where growth almost *never* stops, as in southern California or Florida, or certain Gulf areas, is there but one *proper* time for planting. That's when the weather is as cold as it's likely to get, and bushes are as dormant as they're likely to be. In such places you don't have a very wide choice of planting time. It adds up really to a matter of suitable weeks, not a choice of seasons.

About Soils and pH

Roses are amazingly tolerant of various soil types from sandy to clayey, and of degrees of acidity from pH 4.5 to 7.5, if soil naturally contains plenty of organic matter or it is added in the form of rotted manure, leafmold, peatmoss, etc. The preferred acidity for roses seems to be 5.5 to 6.5. Neutral soils, as you probably know, test pH 7. If soil is too sweet, well above the neutral 7, as it might be, for instance, in Arizona or Utah, foliage will show a yellow or white mottling, evidence of chlorosis. If soil is too sour, far below the neutral 7 and with little organic matter, as it might be in some seashore regions of New Jersey, plants will be stunted and fail to bloom well.

Very likely your soil is fine for roses just as it is. Use it so unless failures with other plants make you suspect trouble. In that case ask your county agricultural agent to test it.

Send soil samples taken from the various places on your property where you plan to plant roses. And for goodness' sake don't start a blind correction program based on liberal applications of lime. That way you'll probably ruin perfectly good soil.

Here the casual gardener really has it over the earnest one who makes a project of everything and does it all the hard way. The lazy gardener digs holes some Saturday and plants his Climbing Roses. Then he waters them well and *fairly* faithfully the first summer, ties them up, fertilizes once the next spring, perhaps, and otherwise lets them alone. So they grow and bloom and everybody admires them. Why don't you be this way? Or at most, spread a 2-inch layer of some "organic matter," as well-rooted or dehydrated manure, peatmoss, leafmold, or compost over the planting area and spade it in a couple of weeks before you plan to plant. It isn't necessary to add any fertilizer at this point.

Difficult Soils

Only if your soil is the rarely-impossible kind for roses should you work very hard over it. When necessary, remove it from each planting hole and combine it half and half with one of the organic materials suggested above. Add also about a cup of a "complete" fertilizer made up for roses or other plants, mixing it all up well before you return it to the hole and plant.

If you want roses at the seashore where your cottage stands apparently in pure sand, follow George E. Lippincott's successful plan. He "plants" climbers each in a peach basket of rich humus and earth. "This rich soil," he writes, "is not obtainable at the shore. Plants are station-wagoned there, a hole dug in the sand for each, the basket kicked in. In about a year and a half the wood of the basket rots away. The rose has become established and thrives. Experience taught me this trick. I found that a hole dug and filled with topsoil didn't last. I've dumped a hundred-pound bag of peatmoss on the sand one day and had most of it disappear by next morning—sieved right down in the sand. The peach-basket idea can also be used on a rocky hillside where erosion is a factor. It works."

There has been plenty of fantastic advice given—and taken —on the preparation of soil and the planting of roses. I saw a handsome specimen of Golden Climber (Mrs. Arthur Curtiss James) flourishing in its twentieth year in a place where soil had been elaborately prepared to a 3-foot depth. Well, my plant of the same variety in its fifth year looks pretty handsome too, and it had only a 12-inch hole, the average topsoil of the site, and yearly fertilizing—also a set-back due to rough handling by painters, but that is another matter. I was told it gave the painters pretty rough handling too!

In most places, you will do well by your climbers if you spade-up and loosen for each one a planting hole about 12 inches deep and 18 inches or so across *as each root spread indicates*. Don't ever wind or cramp or break roots to fit a given space, and, if any are accidentally damaged in packing or planting, cut them *sharply* off just above the bruised or broken area. Do the same for damaged tops, but don't prune canes severely just for the sake of pruning. The grower tended to that when he stored and packaged. You may as well benefit from as extensive growth as he could provide. This goes for dormant plants, of course.

If you are setting out potted or canned roses, remove each container carefully so as to keep the ball of earth unbroken. Set the plant at the same depth it grew before, or a little deeper. Fill in with loose soil which will be an encourage-

ment to growth as roots reach out from the old earth-ball.
Potted roses are easiest to handle if soil is moist, not soggy or
so dry it tends to fall away from roots.

Depth and Distance Apart

Now comes the matter of planting depth—that is, how low
to set the "bud-union," which you will see on each climber
as a knotlike structure above the roots. This is the point
where one kind of root, or understock, usually *Rosa multiflora,* has been joined to another kind of top. The top may
be Noisette, Polyantha, Hybrid Tea, or a variety of very
mixed heritage, but always with less power to root as quickly
or as strongly as the understock on which it is budded.

The American Rose Society advises that the bud-union
"should be at or slightly below the soil level." Walter D.
Brownell wants his hybrid climbers planted with bud-union
3 inches down so "own roots" will form. Where winters are
very cold, 2 inches down has generally proved to be satisfactory. In temperate climates, especially on the West Coast,
many enthusiasts insist the bud union should always be above
ground, where they claim it is far less subject to attacks of
disease. Above-ground planting has other advantages too:
Suckers are easily identified because you can *see* whether
they are coming from roots or top. However, in cold climates

---

*IV. Unwrap plants. Cut back any broken or bruised roots.
Prune back to sound growth any damaged tops, but don't shorten
unnecessarily. Put plants in a pail of water set in the shade.*

*Prepare the planting hole 12 inches deep, 18 inches or so across,
large enough for spreading roots straight out. If an upright support is needed, set this in beforehand. Shape the loosened soil in
the hole into a cone; pat it firm.*

*Set the plant on top of the cone, with the knob or bud-union
just at or slightly below the soil surface; spread the roots out over
it. If there is an extra long root, channel out room for it. Tuck
soil in around the roots, firming well to avoid air pockets.*

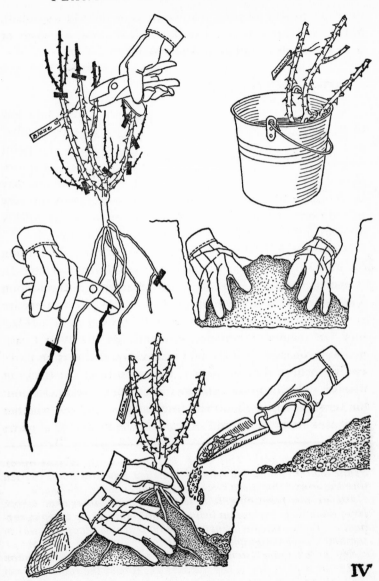

IV

an above-ground bud-union has to be covered in winter where a below-ground one often doesn't. I've had success both ways, and I imagine in many places it doesn't matter, but when winters are zero-cold or colder, I'd rather have the bud-union underground.

As for distances apart, remember almost all climbers are likely to have extensive futures. Better allow each one a 6-foot spread if you are planting along a fence or on a row of pillars; 25 feet isn't too much if you live in a particularly benign growing area like Florida, the Gulf States, or on the Pacific Coast.

Handling Before Planting

If possible, set out plants the day they arrive. Should this be impossible, open each bundle as soon as you can and examine the packing. If it feels nice and moist, wrap up the plants again and put the bundles in a cool place until you are ready to plant—which I hope will be soon.

If the packing feels dry, remove and soak it in water (it is probably sphagnum moss). Then squeeze it out, repack, and wrap up the plants again. Roots protected in this way will not suffer in a cool place so you can safely delay planting for six or seven days, till the week end, say, if the package comes on Monday. Should a long delay be necessary, as when

---

V. Add enough soil to fill the hole three-quarters full; tamp or tramp it firm. Flood the hole with water. Let it drain away. Be sure the lowest roots are well moistened.

Fill in the remaining soil, letting it come somewhat above ground level. It will sink a little. Do not re-water, or tamp again. Remove the tie-on label. Insert a stake with the permanent label.

Protect each spring-planted *climber for one week with an inverted peach basket; remove it every night, replacing it in the morning.*

Cover each fall-planted *bush with a protective mound of soil— the higher it goes, the more wood is likely to be saved for spring.*

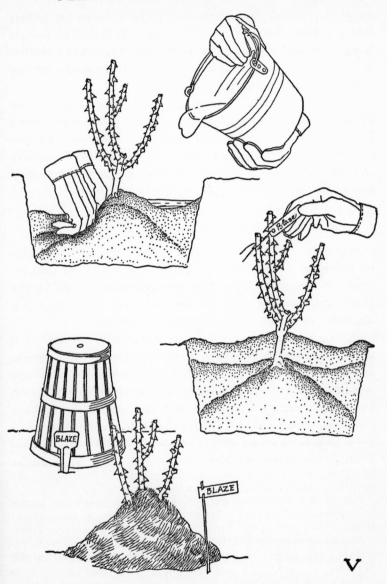

weather is hazardous for weeks, or you have to be away,
better heel-in the plants for the duration. I consider heeling-
in almost more trouble than setting out permanently, but if
you have a vegetable patch where soil is already loosened,
I suppose the process isn't too bad.

For heeling-in roses, prepare a 12-inch-deep trench in a
preferably shaded place. Unpack the plants and spread them
along the trench at a 45-degree angle. Take care that labels
are well attached or make yourself a notebook-list of varieties
in order of placement in the trench. Cover completely with
soil whether the temporary burial is to last for a number of
winter months, or for only a few spring weeks.

Labeling

When you finally plant for good, *do* remove the grower's
label. It won't be long before expanding growth will cause
it to girdle the cane and cause trouble. Better get it off while
you think of it. Then attach a new label to a stake and insert
beside each plant, or get those excellent Perfect Labels which
are T-shaped with plenty of room for you to write variety
and date on a surface that will hold your lead-pencil notation
indefinitely. I like various other permanent labels, too,
especially those of aluminum that you can write on. The
important elements of a label are a large enough surface to
hold important notations—and those permanently—and a
stake or standard for inserting in soil. No tie-on labels,
please!

How to Plant

On the old-but-still-good Chinese theory that one look is
worth a thousand tells, I will now spare the words and suggest
that you examine the easy, step-by-step method of planting
shown here in Drawings IV and V.

CHAPTER ❦ ELEVEN

Culture Is Simple

CLIMBING ROSES are easy to grow, and there is really no reason to make a great to-do about most of them. Depending on heritage, they are more or less demanding, more or less hardy. On every hand, however, there are examples of their terrific powers of survival under neglect.

I think, for instance, of those old climbers I mentioned which flower every spring at a nearby farm. They have been there years and years, covering outbuildings and fences and putting on a grand show early every summer. I *know* they are never sprayed, watered, or fed, and, since bouquets of them are often brought to my house, I've had opportunity to see their excellent flowers close at hand.

And how about the pink and red Ramblers growing everywhere on arbors and fences and creeping over rocks? No one bothers about them. Even at Nantucket where they cover the housetops, no one runs around with a spray gun. Once in a while, in desperation, somebody does a big pruning job, I suppose, so as to maintain a livable balance between the family inside and the ambitious climbers outside, but there is certainly no careful "program" responsible for one of the biggest flower shows on earth.

Then there are the many railroad embankments glorified by the Ramblers. Their blooming is a sight I look forward to every year in late June and early July. The plants clamber 20 to 30 feet among the gray rocks with clumps of wild white daisies among them. If the railroad company does anything about those roses, I'd surely be surprised, knowing this particular railroad as I do.

Generally, however, we want a degree of refinement from the climbers on our houses and fences which are subject to close inspection. We ask for more than stubborn survival. But even when cherished, their needs are minimal; the plants so undemanding and rewarding, that their care is only a pleasure.

Fertilizing

First there is the matter of extra feeding. Since no fertilizer need be applied at planting time, whether that was spring or fall, 3 to 4 inches of growth the *next* spring is the first signal for attention. But keep in mind *roses are not heavy feeders*. They are harmed, not benefited, by the big dose.

Spread a 2-inch layer of aging cow manure around each climber in spring—if that peerless product is available to you. Otherwise apply one of the commercial dehydrated manures which you can buy by the bag; or for established climbers provide half to three-quarters of a cup—depending on size and age—of an "all-purpose" commercial fertilizer. You can buy a package or bag of this in garden-supply or hardware stores, or a container of it to apply in liquid form.

You will find some products labeled 5-10-5 or 4-12-4. Either will suit your roses very well. The numbers refer of course to amounts of the main elements included, as 5 percent of nitrogen, 10 percent of phosphoric acid, and 5 percent of potash. There may also be mysterious references to "trace elements." These are all to the good, but what I like best to see is a statement that the nitrogen content is largely from "organic sources," especially if soil is rather lacking in humus.

If you apply manure, work it *lightly* into the topsoil. The fine feeding roots of roses come quite near the surface, though early in the growing year they are not likely to be injured by the cultivation necessary to incorporate manure into topsoil. But never let manure or any fertilizer come in contact with canes or foliage. It may burn.

If you apply a commercial plant food, spread it over the surface soil. Then work it lightly into the soil and water well to be sure the food goes down and is not carried away by spring wind. There are also excellent plant foods that have been developed just for roses. If you buy one of these, apply according to the manufacturer's directions—though perhaps not so often!

This spring meal may well end the feeding business until another year, particularly for plants set out in soil of average fertility and well-prepared at planting time. Certainly a single feeding suffices for once-blooming climbers, unless these actually show signs of hunger in the course of the next six weeks. Poor color of foliage may be an indication, particularly mottling, paleness to yellowing, gray-greenness on a variety which should be dark green. Even browning of leaves or petal margins could indicate starvation. But dryness, spray or dust burns, unchecked insect attacks or disease produce similar symptoms. You have to develop a little judgment about your climbers. Generally, though, for the once-bloomer, one meal is fine.

Climbing Hybrid Teas, heavy repeat-bloomers like New

Dawn and Blaze, everbloomers like Aloha, Inspiration, Brownell's Everblooming Pillars, or Hybrid Perpetuals, or Hybrid Musks grown as climbers, usually need more food to keep their show definitely on the road. When the first heavy flowering is past, give them a second feeding, and, a month later, a third if you wish, but none after August first, except in warm regions where roses in December are a possibility. Then the third feeding might well be delayed until late August or early September. And be very sure to water plant food in well since the summer season is often dry.

Cultivation and Mulching

Right after the early spring feeding and cultivation, by all means apply a 2- to 3-inch mulch to each climber, if you are growing a number of them. (A mulch is just a covering for the soil of some organic material like buckwheat hulls or peatmoss.) Without a mulch there are weeds to pull and repeated cultivations necessary to break up soil-caking and provide aeration for roots.

I simply can't imagine not mulching, once you discover the beneficent effects. Mulches do so much, and the bother is slight and occurs only once a year, or even once in several years. A mulch lets you be lazy. When I use buckwheat hulls, I just *pour* them from the bag to about a 3-inch depth around each plant. What could be simpler? And then the mulch stays (this one for three to four years), discouraging weeds, reducing evaporation of soil moisture, preventing crusting-over of the earth, and reducing blackspot, whose spores flourish when splashed by rain onto bare soil.

Mulches disintegrate sooner or later so you never have to remove them. Some, like ground corncobs, even add a little fertility, and eventually improve soil by increasing friability or sponginess. And with a mulch there's no danger of injuring surface roots by summer hoeing, since you don't have to cultivate. Once in a while a determined weed pops through the mulch, but you can always pull it out easily on one of your admiring evening strolls, and when you do, you will be pleased, as I always am, to feel the moist condition of the soil beneath.

If you give a second or third fertilizing to your busy repeaters, first scrape the mulch aside. Then feed, water well, and rake the mulch back in place. It's all very easy.

Enthusiasts who use mulches swear by them, but not all by the same ones. Many of us use peatmoss. I prefer it for climbers around the house. Peatmoss has such a neat look and turns such a handsome, comfortable brown when wet. However, it is more expensive than most other types.

If you use peatmoss, first soak it well. I always order my bale early, and stand it outside by the garage with the top open to catch early-spring rains. If these aren't heavy enough to moisten the peatmoss thoroughly by the time I am ready to spread it, I lay a slow-running hose on top of the opened bale and let it go long enough to saturate. *Dry* peatmoss can be a liability. If rains do not occur right after it is spread, it will draw from the soil all the moisture available to satisfy its greed for water—and so actually *rob* the plant. Once soaked, peatmoss behaves just fine as a mulch.

Other possibilities for mulches are: fairly well-decomposed leaves or compost or manure (not pretty, but healthy and satisfactory), lawn clippings and straw (both very messy), sawdust (for safe use should be three years old; attractive and cheap), ground corncobs (easy and satisfactory), rice or cottonseed hulls, or peanut shells (unattractive for near view), and spent tanbark, pine needles, or redwood bark—all excellent where available.

Partway through the summer, you may want to add to the mulch. It depends on the material you use and also on the

weather. Some mulches decompose and some at times wash
away with very heavy rains. I never have to add to peatmoss
or buckwheat hulls, but I allow nearer a 3- than a 2-inch
depth right at the start. Because the buckwheat hulls last
so long, you can, where winters are severe, place a 15-inch-
wire cylinder around each climber and heap up more buckwheat hulls inside the cylinder.

Watering

Nothing promotes the health of Climbing Roses more than
plenty of water. The first growing season after planting,
they are particularly dependent on moisture since the root
system has not yet developed good foraging ability. I am
always amazed at the trouble people will go to for roses—
deep soil preparation, heavy feeding, constant spraying—but
do they tend religiously to watering, no!

The main reasons for this neglect is faith in rainfall, and
dependence on it. Yet too often it happens that it "looks
like rain" for weeks, but never does. Even if you wait for
rain and get it, it may only be enough to moisten an inch or
so of the soil. That's no use to an established climber. It
needs thorough wetting, 8 inches or so deep, and that about
every two weeks in normal seasons, every week if one of
those really droughty spells occurs.

The best way to be sure of thorough watering is to place
a *slow-running* hose beside each climber and let it stay there
for half an hour to an hour. Then poke your fingers into the
soil, and test it for dryness, if you have doubts. Keep in
mind soaking down to 8 inches is the goal. If a soil channel
develops, press the earth back with your foot.

Overhead watering is no good (unless foliage is actually
dusty). First of all it takes forever for a water spray to soak
soil, and meanwhile the wet foliage is a wide-open invitation

to mildew and blackspot. If you must water from above, at least do it mornings so the sun will quickly dry the leaves. Sprinkling in the evening to amuse and cool yourself, is a downright wicked practice, so far as your roses are concerned. Wet foliage at night usually means fungous trouble in the morning. All of which lands me—where I am always loath to go—at the subject of pest and disease.

Control of Pest and Disease

With roses we can't avoid this subject but we certainly don't have to make a fetish of it either, particularly with climbers. I am sure if, when I first planted roses, I had known as much as I know now of the supposed hazards of growing them, I wouldn't have set out a single one. As it is, I now grow mostly climbers because they don't begin to require the amount of protection the majority of bush roses do, and that goes even for the Climbing Hybrid Teas. Certainly very few of us do anything about spraying American Pillar or a great Silver Moon covering the side of a house. Also I have discovered that Climbing Roses have more ability to cope with trouble by themselves than we usually give them credit for.

Indeed, that's true of many plants. I remember "The Case of the Copper Beech," planted quite close to my house in Philadelphia. The first spring I lived there I noticed a terrific infestation of aphids. The "tree-man" quoted a price of twenty-five dollars for spraying. Since I didn't have twenty-five dollars for a spray job that spring, I let the tree carry on alone. And it did, growing so much that the side of the stone house seemed almost endangered by its power. In the next years, I discovered that monstrous tree *always* had twenty-five dollars worth of aphids in spring, and *always* survived them, unaided by me.

Now Climbing Roses aren't copper beech trees, though many a one, like a tree, has survived for generations, long outliving the man who planted it. But if ever you have had to neglect your climbers for some emergency, you know how well most of them stood the strain. And certainly there are notable types with enough Wichuraiana ancestry to produce tough, glossy leaves that are never bothered by *anything*, hence my deep and abiding affection for American Pillar, City of York, Carpet of Gold, Little Compton Creeper, and their kin.

Also I know one enthusiast—who shall be nameless—who thoroughly enjoys some twenty climbers growing in a variety of situations on her place, but none very high up. Each year she buys a sifter can of all-purpose rose dust, and that's it. Coverage is poor and not always timely, but her roses look pretty nice and give her a great deal of pleasure. She is not one for plant coddling, being a thrower-outer of exacting varieties. With such casual attention, however, Paul's Scarlet, Golden Climber, Dr. J. H. Nicolas, Mary Wallace, Dr. W. Van Fleet, Silver Moon, and various trailers put on a very lovely show indeed.

For you who are more exacting, or, perhaps I should say for you who grow more *exacting varieties,* the regular weekly spraying schedule is perhaps a good thing. Start in spring when first leaves unfurl and keep it up till frost—if you have the strength. After the first important protective spray in spring, however, you could wait for signs of trouble, aphids next most likely, before getting out the dusting or spraying equipment again and going to it.

The all-purpose sprays (I like Tri-ogen very much), and dusts, which I prefer to sprays, are such a comfort because you don't have to decide what to do for what, no diagnosing, no prescribing required. Blackspot, mildew, canker, rust— aphids (plant lice), mites, thrips, beetles, rose bugs, all the nasty sucking and chewing insects—are pretty well controlled or incapacitated by the carefully-made preparations now available. These tend to be more expensive than specific materials for specific ailments because part of the time you are using controls for troubles that have not occurred or are not likely to, but the one material is prepared to combat everything.

If you prefer to mix your own, you can prepare a *dust* to use *only* when temperatures are below 90 degrees F. (sulphur burns in high heat), of:

9 parts fine dusting sulphur

1 part powdered lead arsenate (Poison)

1 part nicotine dust, added only when plant lice cluster on new growth.

Cover plants *lightly,* but thoroughly, leaf surfaces and underneath. Or you can, in the same thorough way, apply a *spray:*

2 teaspoons Dreft (or other detergent for spreading) dissolved in:

6 gallons of water, with

3 tablespoons wettable sulphur

50 percent wettable DDT

Apply either on a regular weekly schedule to your Hybrid Tea or other more delicate climbers, so as to maintain a constant protective film. Or watch plants and apply as needed, which is usually less often in hot, dry weather when there is no rain to wash off spray or dust. If aphids cluster on young leaves and buds, as they are likely to in spring, dust with the nicotine added. If leaves look spotty, pick off affected ones (burn them), and then dust or spray, and repeat at intervals. If mildew attacks, as it usually does the Ramblers, especially when days are warm and nights cool, and if they are overgrown or shaded, dust or spray but, as I said, not on a very hot day. Wait for a temperature drop.

I prefer dusting because it's so much less of a chore, and I advise it because I know many busy people who *will* dust because they can keep a filled duster always at hand, and won't spray because of the mixing of material and washing of equipment required. After all, dusting, done, is far better for plants than spraying only contemplated.

When you buy a duster or sprayer, buy a good one. A well-made one lasts a long time. A cheap one does a poor job and is no fun to handle.

Also be comforted by the fact that *climbers properly set out in places open to sun and air, if kept adequately watered, are not prone to serious infestations.* Plenty of birds are also good insurance against insect damage. Birds and Climbing Roses are an aesthetic combination anyway, and a lovely one I wouldn't be without!

However, if you live in a Japanese-beetle area, even a multitude of birds won't be able to keep up with the possibilities, so you will *have* to do battle with a DDT spray or dust with arsenate of lead or one of the preparations made for beetles, particularly if your climbers are types that bloom in beetle time. One of my neighbors, a landscape architect who grows only the "easy" climbers (and so handsomely; some are nearly 30 years old), never dusts or sprays except in "beetle years." She likes Styx for the purpose because it does the job without discoloring flowers or foliage. If beetles are serious with you, better grow only the once-bloomers.

Wintering the Climbers

In the greater part of this country, and in some sections of Canada, Climbing Roses can be grown without special winter protection. They are a complete joy then for us who never have this particular concern. Even where zero temperatures occur, most climbers come safely through because house-walls or fences serve to protect them. And there are also some with greater cold tolerance, like many of the Brownell varieties, which have successfully withstood as much as 30 degrees below. Even where weather gets zero cold, a 6- to 8-inch mound of soil heaped over roots and the base of the canes suffices. This insures the life of the plant even though in some winters severe top damage may occur. And with roots saved, it doesn't take most climbers long to produce another fine top, since many grow 5 to 15 feet in just one growing season. In very cold places where your more ex- perienced neighbors report damage to climbers, lash ever- green boughs or discarded Christmas trees to the canes to insure safety of all the top growth.

Where temperatures drop regularly to 10 to 20 degrees below, the only course—unless your climbers are of a breed to withstand such cold—is to remove them from the supports. Lay them down on the ground while they are still pliant, fasten them firmly with crossed plant stakes or with heavy wire pegs (wire bent into the form of a croquet wicket), and, *after* a good freeze, in the coldest climates, cover them com- pletely with soil—but only in the coldest. And do bring in extra soil from vegetable garden or annual bed; don't try to scrape it up from around the roots.

Or you can hold down the canes with heavy boards or bricks. Do this as late as possible but while canes can still be bent. Or use a good packing of salt hay, or Fiberglass, re- portedly successful in cold sections of Canada, although it is fairly expensive, if you have many plants, and also rather hard to handle. Avoid leaves or any other soggy covering which will tend to produce canker or rotting.

To be specific then:

Ramblers are safe on their own down to 10 degrees below. Then a soil mound is necessary and the canes should be taken down and pegged to the ground. At 20 degrees below, cover the canes also with soil.

Large-flowered Climbers and repeaters need the soil mound even at zero, and if your climate is colder, protect them the same as the Ramblers.

Climbing Hybrid Teas and *Climbing Floribundas,* as you would expect, are the most tender of the climbers, hardly suited to 20 degrees F. and *usually* requiring, even at zero, a soil mound and the laying down of canes. At 10 degrees below also cover canes with soil. (Some varieties can stand more cold than others.)

Trailers need no winter protection, except perhaps a little mulching in 20-degree-below climates.

Early in spring have the climbers in mind. When the likelihood of a hard freeze seems over, push or wash away the soil mounds. Don't coddle plants too long, for that insulating layer of soil may start them into rather early growth. Get them back on trellises or pillars or fences as soon as weather permits—and you can stand the job. If there's much dealing with canes in view, you want to get it done before new growth may be damaged by the necessary handling.

Be over-early rather than over-late, since climbers can stand a fair amount of cold so long as the pith of the canes is not actually frozen hard. A light freeze, more or less, won't hurt. And if the weather prophets warn of some late, untimely hazard, get out emergency wrappings, burlap bags, even newspapers.

Sometimes field mice cozying down in the mulched plants cause more harm than the cold. To guard against them where plants are heavily covered and canes may be girdled, include one of those poison-grain baits in your plans—but offer it dry. Place it in a soup or fruit-juice can laid on the side with a piece of board placed on top and reaching over the "entrance" to keep out the rain. Set your "traps" in protected strategic spots among the rose canes before you mulch.

If you live in below-zero areas, consider, before you get involved in this bothersome wintering business, whether you shouldn't plant climbers bred to take it uncoddled. Also choose protected locations and experiment a little. Rambler-type climbers and some of the others (but not most of the Climbing Hybrid Teas or Floribundas) might survive the conditions you offer with just a soil mound. Unless you really like an arduous project, I'd advise a little trial and error before you let yourself in for an up-and-down project with climbers.

Also keep in mind, the healthy plant, the well-watered plant is always more likely to endure the hazards of winter than sufferers from pest, disease, or drought.

CHAPTER TWELVE

Pruning with Purpose

CLIMBING ROSES as a group need little pruning. Only Rambler-types require much attention.

The first guide to pruning climbers lies in the nature of each plant: Does it naturally grow tall, that is to 20 or 30 feet, or is 7 to 8 feet a likely maximum? Does the variety in question set blooms on new or old wood, on the tips of upright canes or on horizontal growth; does it flower once or repeatedly right up to frost? Is its constitution tough or so tender that winter cold kills it back plenty and you value every bit of live wood in spring?

The second, less important guide lies in the destiny you offer each plant: What do you want it to do? Do you wish it to stay neat and tidy as adornment for pillar or delicate arch, or do you expect it to cover the side of your house or spread out all over a low roof so you can look down on it from upstairs windows? Or are you in hopes it will clamber far over a great rocky outcropping or along a monstrously-long fence? If you plant climbers with growth habits suited to their locations, you will have much less pruning to do than if you try to make varieties of naturally-vigorous constitution play restricted roles.

After the main season of flowering is over—and the only one for Ramblers and once-bloomers—you can attend to any really important pruning you have in mind. As far as health is concerned, however, you can leave most of the climbers alone, unless you have in view special destinies for them. After first flowering, then, is the time to prune—and train— as you see fit.

Suckers

Sucker growth from the base of plants may be hard to identify unless the bud-union is well above ground. It is, of course, growth that emerges from the root-stock on which the choicer climbing variety has been budded. The stock was selected in the first place for its vigor. Sometimes it tries to take over. If allowed to flourish, that's just what it will do, destroying the desirable top by crowding it out.

If an unusually strong cane appears at the base of your Climbing Rose, examine it. It can look somewhat different, especially in color, and still belong, since the young growth of many plants often differs from the old. Usually, however, color and texture of foliage and type of thorns and shoots from the understock are very different. If you aren't sure, first try to determine the source of growth. Suckers start from a point *below* the bud or knob of the union. Suckers from multiflora understock, the one most commonly used, have light-green foliage and clusters of white flowers, if they get that far. Ragged Robin understock, which is considerably used in California, has reddish leaves and a red flower. If you are sure basal growth is from the understock, cut it *out* not simply *off* or it will soon get going again. If necessary, scrape

VI

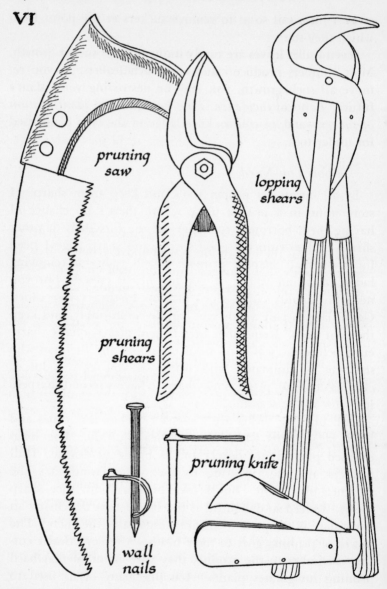

pruning
saw

lopping
shears

pruning
shears

pruning knife

wall
nails

away a little soil so as to remove suckers at the point from which they start.

Seven-leaflet leaves are rarely indications of sucker growth. Most climbers produce canes with such leaflets. If you remove all such growth, you may be destroying your plant's future. *Point of incidence is the best guide to identification of suckers*—and, of course, knowledge of the type plant used for understock.

Tools You Need

By all means get proper tools and keep them sharp. (I store mine in a *private* place where there's no chance of having them borrowed to whack off the forsythias or other shrubs and so ruin the good spring and sharp edge I need for my roses.) Snapcut pruners are all right for removing faded roses and young or not too heavy growth, but you need first-quality curve-edged pruners for heavy rose canes. Get as large a pair as you can handle comfortably, and keep the edge keen. Remember to get them professionally sharpened before the season of use is upon you and the man who sharpens is inundated with work. If you have a lot of climbers to tend, pruners may have to have a second sharpening later in the season.

Dull pruning shears are a menace. They tear canes and leave jagged cuts which do not heal quickly. The long-exposed pith invites borers and is prone to disease. Dull pruners are also revolting to use. They would try the patience of a saint. But I love pruning with nice sharp shears. Indeed so delightful is the occupation that many an enthusiast is tempted to overdo, especially the men. The power of pruning goes to their heads. After practically cutting a climber to the ground, they will maintain that hard pruning invigorates plants. Actually many of us used to believe that.

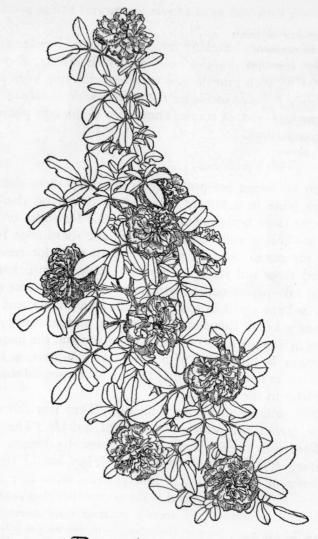

VII Rambler Chevy Chase

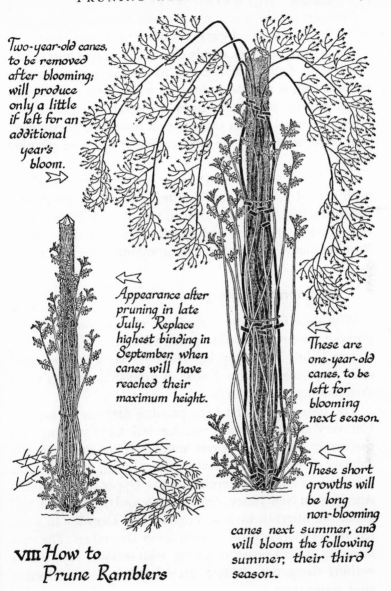

Two-year-old canes, to be removed after blooming; will produce only a little if left for an additional year's bloom. ⇨

⇦ Appearance after pruning in late July. Replace highest binding in September, when canes will have reached their maximum height.

⇦ These are one-year-old canes, to be left for blooming next season.

⇦ These short growths will be long non-blooming canes next summer, and will bloom the following summer, their third season.

VIII How to Prune Ramblers

Now we realize that hard pruning reduces leafage, and leaves are the manufacturers of food. Plants need them.

If you have old, very woody climbers, you may also need a small saw. Canes often prove too heavy for your hand pruners and, if you twist these, to make them cut through tough growth, you'll ruin them—for good. Lopping shears are also essential if a big arch or arbor must be kept trimmed. You could wear out your arm tending it just with pruning shears.

And do get yourself some heavy leather guantlets with a good cuff, if you have much pruning to attend to, as with Ramblers, and wear long sleeves, too. I have known some who tried it in shorts and sports shirt with dire results. Pruning should not be akin to martyrdom; it's really fun!

Early Spring Pruning

With these two guides—the nature of each plant and your purpose concerning it—first prune each climber, *if it needs it,* very lightly in early spring. *Wait for main pruning until after blooming.* Cutting before, if extensive, removes wood that produces flower buds.

The *time* for the first light pruning depends on locality. Cut very sparingly when you see leaf buds swelling and preferably before the leaves unfold. This could be late January or early February along the Gulf or in California, a few weeks later in Georgia and the Upper South, around April first in New Jersey, Pennsylvania, and the Midwest, and about the fifteenth in New England and Canada. In some sections of Florida it could even be in December. The date of spring growth varies, of course, with seasons. Also there's nothing dangerous about a little leeway. You *can* prune after leaves open.

The purpose of the early spring pruning is simply to remove wood damaged by weather or disease. Cut back to sound tissue any canes with cankers; cut back to the ground line, if necessary, any dead canes; cut well below any splits in bark which occur when a long branch has been torn away from a main stem by the wind; cut away weak, twiggy growth that thickens up the center of a plant: it has no future. On the whole, *go easy this first time.* You can always do a little supplementary pruning, as you see the full extent of winter damage, if that tends to be considerable in your locality.

If you aren't sure about the true condition of a cane, wait a little and watch behavior. Generally, damaged wood is darker than normal for a variety, but sound old wood may also be dark colored. In spring most healthy wood is rather light green or yellowish. Healthy pith is normally white; if it is brown, keep cutting back till you reach a section with white pith.

When you cut across a cane that is larger, say, than a lead pencil, it is wise to protect the cut area. (Some climbers, especially the yellows of foetida parentage, will positively die if *every* wound is not covered.) Expose as little pith as possible, of course, by making only *slightly* slanting cuts. Then smear these with tree paint—an asphalt compound is best—or shellac or, if there are only a few cut canes to protect, cover each with a little wad of chewing gum.

If you must, also prune now a little for shapeliness, but operate with a light hand. Keep in mind, *when you prune away sound growth in spring, you are removing flowering wood.* Can your climbers spare it and do you wish to reduce the crop for the sake of conformity perhaps to arch or fence rail? Often such regulation of growth is well worth while for the overall looks of a plant, but generally you should wait until after first flowering. My point is, when you prune, know what you are doing—and why.

IX *Paul's Scarlet Climber*

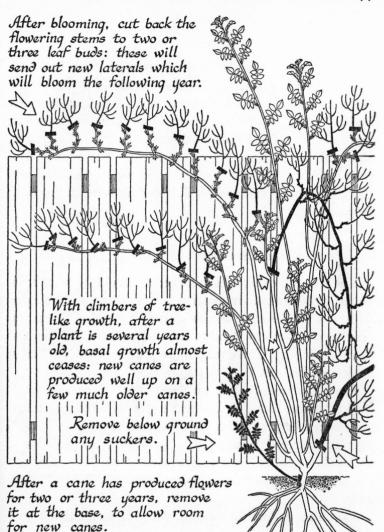

After blooming, cut back the flowering stems to two or three leaf buds: these will send out new laterals which will bloom the following year.

With climbers of tree-like growth, after a plant is several years old, basal growth almost ceases: new canes are produced well up on a few much older canes.

Remove below ground any suckers.

After a cane has produced flowers for two or three years, remove it at the base, to allow room for new canes.

x-How to Prune Once-blooming Large-flowered Climbers

How to Prune

When you prune, always cut back close to a leaf bud. Don't slice into it, and don't cut so far above it you leave a piece of stem to rot, as when a cut is made halfway between buds. Try to cut about a quarter-inch above. Let the cut point outward if you want to develop open, fanwise growth. Slant the cut in if there's an open space that needs a new cane to fill it. But don't be too concerned about this; you can always *train* new growth if it doesn't start in the right direction.

Pruning the Ramblers

The old-fashioned, cluster-flowered Ramblers, with individual blossoms usually under 2 inches, often produce 15 to 20 feet of pliable canes in one season. Typical of this group are the pink Dorothy Perkins, red Chevy Chase, and Sanders' White Rambler. These need more pruning than the Large-flowered Climbers.

Ramblers produce best on year-old wood, so this year's choice blooms come on last year's growth. And one year's growth can be prodigious! Unless space is no object and a plant can spread tremendously, as over a low roof on a Nantucket cottage or an outcropping of New England boulders, a Rambler needs severe cutting back fairly regularly.

Soon after a Rambler blooms, you will notice that a considerable number of strong new shoots are under way at the base—already 3 feet long perhaps. The recommended practice is to remove Ramblers yearly from their supports, lay them on the ground, and cut out all the old canes right at the ground line. Then tie up the new canes as in Drawing VIII. But what a job!

Actually, if you cut out *some* of the old canes (which also bear a small amount of flowers), every year, or *all* of the old ones every second or third year, depending on available space and thickness of growth, you will still be able to keep your Ramblers from turning into thorny thickets, as they too often do. The remedy for this condition, of course, is to chop down the plants completely and let them start all over again. You can't separate new canes from old at the thicket stage, so better not let Ramblers reach it.

When you do remove old canes, deal with them piecemeal. Instead of making but one cut at the ground line and pulling out each enormous cane all in one piece—which, suddenly released, can practically knock you flat—cut across the canes you are removing every 8 inches or so. Most of the small pieces will then fall out, and you can easily pull out the sticklers by catching hold of them with your pruners. Raking up the pieces is simple compared to all-in-one removal of a giant cane.

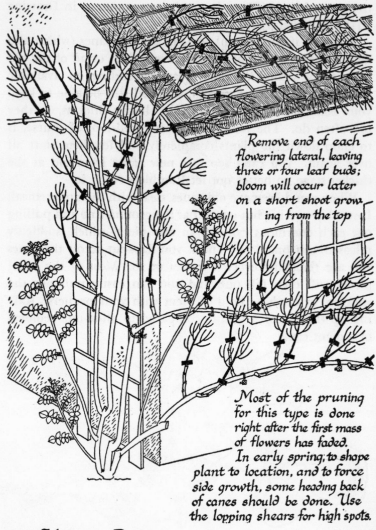

Remove end of each
flowering lateral, leaving
three or four leaf buds;
bloom will occur later
on a short shoot grow-
ing from the top

Most of the pruning
for this type is done
right after the first mass
of flowers has faded.
In early spring, to shape
plant to location, and to force
side growth, some heading back
of canes should be done. Use
the lopping shears for high spots.

XI—How to Prune
Repeat-blooming Large-flowered Climbers

XII

New Dawn

Pruning Once-blooming Large-flowered Types

Don't let pruning prey on your mind. Too often conscientious, but inexperienced, gardeners read in the newspaper garden pages and periodicals the usual June counsel to prune Climbing Roses. This is timely advice but like all generalities, it must be interpreted in terms of *your* roses. And maybe yours need very little pruning, especially if they are quite young or very old. Canes of the Large-flowered Climbers are not so pliable as those on Ramblers, and, as plants mature, fewer new canes spring up from the base.

Typical of this class are the red Bess Lovett, Dr. Huey, Paul's Scarlet Climber, and Thor; the pink Dr. W. Van Fleet, Mary Wallace, and Mme. Gregoire Staechelin; the white City of York and Silver Moon; and the yellow Doubloons, Elegance, and Golden Climber. (See Drawing X.)

If any of these are grown for a neat, definite pattern, as on a long fence or perhaps espaliered against a house, after first bloom is over they may require considerable pruning. The amount depends, as always, on chosen manner of growth, and space. Usually there is side growth that needs to be cut off in order to keep plants flat where *you* want them so.

On most once-bloomers, prune all you feel like right after flowering and repeat the job if it should be required through the summer. *This year's flowers will usually be produced on the side shoots or laterals that grow out from the old wood.* After flowering cut these back to 5 to 15 inches. Let them stay long and train them if you want a *broad* display.

When plants of the Large-flowering once-bloomers are well established, but not before, it will be time enough to consider taking out perhaps a third of the oldest canes at the base, or maybe just one of them. Since many choice climbers in this class hardly come into their own before the third year after planting, don't consider removing canes until then—and maybe not till the fifth year.

Before you do so, ask yourself, has my Silver Moon, Dr. W. Van Fleet, or Paul's Scarlet (1) grown out of bounds, or (2) are some of the canes not producing well? A yes-answer to either would indicate some cane-removal at the base, particularly if the plant was long established and there were rather dark, woody-looking canes that bore sparsely. Always keep in mind *you prune mainly to keep plants sufficiently renewed for good flower production*. Types vary in the production quality of old and new wood.

Some once-bloomers like Golden Climber (Mrs. Arthur Curtiss James) and Silver Moon produce treelike growth which should make an enthusiastic pruner go easy. On these there is much less new basal growth than on Ramblers, for instance, and flowers are freely produced from old wood.

The thing we all have to do is to know our own particular climbers. I repeat: Many take at least three years to become established. In the case of Golden Climber, just mentioned, that is certainly so. Also its flowers come not on laterals but on stems from these, that is, on sub-laterals. Too often there is disappointment with this truly handsome climber because people get impatient with it, train it straight up, not sidewise as it requires, and prune it much too drastically.

I cut very little from my now five-year plant except to keep it from growing across a window. I've allotted to it half the front of the house and am encouraging it to spread over the little portico of the front door too. After canes are trained up, they are leveled off so as to develop many sub-laterals open to sun and air. Even some of the faded blossoms are left so handsome seed hips can develop for autumn display.

If you want neater plants in the after-bloom weeks, cut back the flower clusters (of once-bloomers) to 4 to 6 inches. But don't do that on the repeat climbers we are going to talk about next, or you will destroy lots of developing flower buds.

XIII *Climbing Crimson Glory*

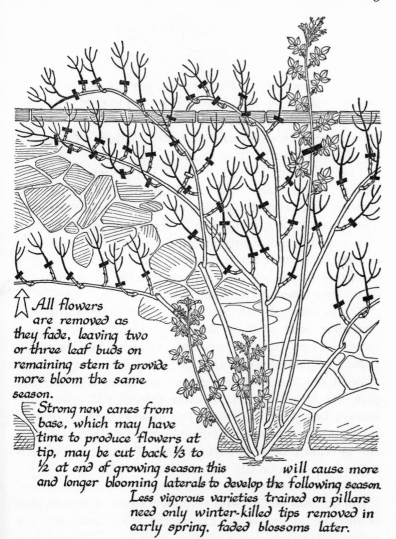

All flowers are removed as they fade, leaving two or three leaf buds on remaining stem to provide more bloom the same season.

Strong new canes from base, which may have time to produce flowers at tip, may be cut back ⅓ to ½ at end of growing season: this will cause more and longer blooming laterals to develop the following season. Less vigorous varieties trained on pillars need only winter-killed tips removed in early spring, faded blossoms later.

XIV-How to Prune Climbing Hybrid Teas

Pruning Repeat or Ever-blooming Climbers

Some climbers bloom off and on during the summer and then heavily in the fall. They are the repeaters, a variable group on production. Among them are the red Blaze (the newest strain much more productive than the old), the pink Dr. J. H. Nicolas, Dream Girl, Inspiration, Parade, and New Dawn; the yellow Mermaid and Mrs. Whitman Cross; and the white Prosperity. (See Drawing XI.)

The Climbing Hybrid Teas, like Crimson Glory and Paul's Lemon Pillar, and the Climbing Polyanthas, like Summer Snow and Goldilocks, bloom fairly steadily. The group known as Brownell's Everblooming Pillars are very constant, producing amazing amounts of flowers on every tip of growth, and these set no blind canes. Prune only to keep plants shapely and ornamental in the place allotted to them. (See Drawings XIV and XVI.)

If you grow any of these repeat or constant climbers, remember *most of them shudder at the sight of pruning shears*. Their balance between vegetative and flowering growth is naturally delicate. Furthermore, many of them (though not the Brownell group) are more winter-tender than the once-bloomers, so some growth will usually be winterkilled. Cut that back to live wood at the time of early spring pruning; prune in summer only to keep plants shapely and to remove faded flowers. Unless, of course, you are trying to keep to pillar-size varieties like New Dawn or Jacotte which then must be headed back two or three times a season.

Cut off dead blooms with very *short* stems. The next crop of roses comes out of the axil of the first normal leaf just below the fading flower cluster. Cut just a quarter-inch above this. Get rid of withered flowers well before they start turning into seed pods, and preferably before they shatter and petals fall.

Pruning Shrubs or Could-be Climbers and the Trailers

Little pruning is necessary for any of these except as you wish to shape them to your purpose along a fence, to thin them for productive growth, which will necessitate some removal of canes (perhaps a fourth of them each year) on older plants, and, of course, removal of any winterkilled wood, which won't be much.

Trailing Roses like Carpet of Gold, Max Graf, Coral Creeper, and *Rosa Wichuraiana* itself require almost nothing: a little thinning perhaps and removal of any dead branches.

By no means remove faded flowers from Shrubs or trailers. There is a handsome crop of black, scarlet, or orange hips possible from all of them, lovely for autumn and Christmas decoration. Let these develop for a second glory.

How to Cut Flowers for the House

While climbers are small, control your urge to cut roses for bouquets and arrangements. At first, plants need all possible vegetative growth. Most of them have a long way to grow; they need all the leaves they produce if their efforts at tall growing are to be properly nourished. Therefore cut roses on young plants no further back than the first normal leaflets. With the short-stemmed roses you can make floating arrangements, using foliage from other plants. Even when Climbing Hybrid Teas and Climbing Floribundas are well developed, be sparing with stem-cutting; long stems mean fewer flowers so you must make a choice.

Well-grown Ramblers and other once-bloomers you can, of course, cut by the armful, and what a joy that will be.

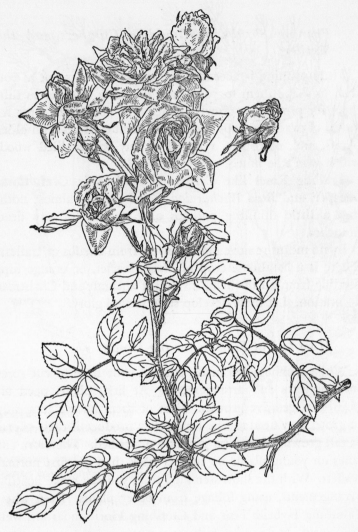

xv *Climbing Goldilocks*

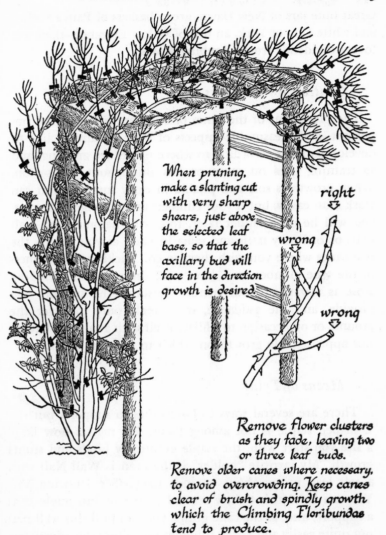

When pruning, make a slanting cut with very sharp shears, just above the selected leaf base, so that the axillary bud will face in the direction growth is desired.

right

wrong

wrong

Remove flower clusters as they fade, leaving two or three leaf buds.

Remove older canes where necessary, to avoid overcrowding. Keep canes clear of brush and spindly growth which the Climbing Floribundas tend to produce.

XVI- How to Prune Climbing Floribundas

Great blue jars of New Dawn, green baskets of Paul's Scarlet and white City of York, an urn of yellow Elegance—these are lovely dividends from Climbing Roses.

Controls for Climbers

The placement of the canes of climbers is one of the important—and pleasurable—aspects of their culture. I like to develop patterns according to where plants are growing, and so training goes on more or less throughout the season. When growth is soft and pliable in early summer, you can work most easily, but if your climbers are tall, vigorous types, you will be on a ladder later, too, with hammer and wall nails or ordinary nails and raffia in hand as you deploy the stiff canes where you wish them to go. Lacking the adjuncts of the true climber, as I have said, the so-called *Climbing* Rose is always at your mercy. Without the support *you* provide, and the guidance, it is likely only to cover the ground, or on occasion to affiliate itself with a tall tree having low approachable growth on which to start an ascent.

Means of Tying

There are several ways to hold canes to supports but the U-shaped staple is not among them. No matter how large a size you start with, the staple eventually binds and stunts growth. My favorite "holder" is the Francis Wall Nail with a soft lead prong about an inch long. (See Drawing VI.) You can bend this tightly around a cane or just angle it as a support; also, as the cane grows, you can pull this wall nail out quite easily and fasten it higher up. This is an advantage, since it is not an inexpensive gadget and furthermore it does rust. Even so, for fastening a Climbing Rose directly against a house (which I do as know I shouldn't!), this wall nail is my pet. Ordinary nails with a small loop of twine fastened around the head and a bigger loop around the cane work well, too.

Whenever a cane is fastened, it is wise to do the tying first—to pole, rail, or whatever—and then the loose looping around the cane. There should always be sufficient leeway for a cane to move a little. A binding tie will bruise and even cut.

Generally used for tying canes are jute, raffia, narrow strips of cloth, and I also like a paper-bound wire called Twist-N-Tye. It comes on a great cardboard spool and is easily cut by clippers without ruining the edge. I use this bound wire for fastening canes around upright fence posts or drawing canes fanwise or horizontally to the rails and holding them there while growth is too short to reach. For trellis-growers this wire is useful, too.

Methods of Training

In training climbers it is, as I have said, important to know the nature of each one. Unless varieties are designated as pillars and are capable of bloom on tall upright growth, you will be very disappointed in their performance if you so train them. The Climbing Hybrid Teas and Climbing Floribundas do well on pillars, so do Blaze, Dr. J. H. Nicolas, Pink Cloud, Parade, and many more. But many climbers bloom better if the greater part of the growth is placed horizontally. It is possible, of course, even with Golden Climber, to take canes straight up to a first floor roof, say, and *then* spread them out; only so will the plant really bloom, and how magnificently!

When you want a neat job, almost an espalier—as I prefer all vines—train and attach canes on the *outside* of the plant to the *lowest* part of the trellis, or run them a little way along the foundation of the house. Then fasten the inner canes higher up so that they travel vertically a short distance before they assume the side- or fan-wise line. Actually you can develop quite an exact horizontal pattern on a post-and-rail or post-and-board fence if you have the patience—and enjoy the task as I do. And how those horizontal canes bloom, especially on Shrub Roses grown as climbers, and Inspiration along a fence produces 15- to 18-inch stems.

Once a tall-growing plant is well established, unless space is unlimited, you cannot *train* all the vigorous canes it produces at the base (these are rarely suckers), so you will discover that training-plus-pruning tends to be a delightful summer-long occupation.

MASTER LIST OF CLIMBING ROSES

All of the species and varieties listed below are available today from one or more of the growers given on page 198 ff. See Chapter 7 for *more* Shrubs which may be grown as climbers and are often considered as such.

Adelaide d'Orleans. Semp.
Albéric Barbier. LC
Albertine. LC
Alida Lovett. LC
Alister Stella Gray. N
Allen's Golden Climber. LC
Aloha. CHT
American Pillar. LC
Amethyst. R
Apeles Mestres. CHP
Apricot Glow. LC
Arabian Nights. HMs
Auguste Roussel. LC
Aviateur Blériot. R

Baltimore Belle. HSet
Beauty of Glazenwood (Fortune's Double Yellow; San Rafael Rose). N
Belinda. HMs
Belle Blanca. HG
Belle Portugaise (Belle of Portugal). HG
Bess Lovett. LC
Billy Boiler. CHT
Birdie Blye. C
Black Boy. CHT
Blaze. LC

Bloomfield Courage. R
Bloomfield Dainty. Evbl.-Semi-Cl
Blossomtime. Cl
Bobbink White Climber. LC
Bonfire. R
Brownell Yellow Rambler. R

Captain Thomas. CHT
Carpet of Gold. LC
Cherokee Rose (*R. laevigata*)
Cherub. R
Chevy Chase. R
Chin Chin (Promise). CC
City of York. LC
Cl. Autumn. CHT
Cl. American Beauty. LC
Cl. Best Regards. CHT
Cl. Better Times. CHT
Cl. Break o' Day. CHT
Cl. Briarcliff. CHT
Cl. Caledonia. CHT
Cl. California. CHT
Cl. Capistrano. CHT
Cl. Cécile Brunner. CFl
Cl. Charles P. Kilham. CHT
Cl. Charlotte Armstrong. CHT
Cl. Cherry. CHT
Cl. Christopher Stone. CHT

Cl. Chrysler Imperial. CHT
Cl. Columbia. CHT
Cl. Condesa de Sástago. CHT
Cl. Countess Vandal. CHT
Cl. Crimson Glory. CHT
Cl. "Daily Mail" Scented Rose. CHT
Cl. Dainty Bess. CHT
Cl. Dame Edith Helen. CHT
Cl. Devoniensis (Magnolia Rose). CT
Cl. Duquesa de Peñaranda. CHT
Cl. E. G. Hill. CHT
Cl. Else Poulsen. CFl
Cl. Ena Harkness. CHT
Cl. Etoile de Hollande. CHT
Cl. Feu Joseph Looymans. CHT
Cl. Firebrand. CHT
Cl. Floradora. CFl
Cl. Forty-niner. CHT
Cl. Frau Karl Druschki. CHP
Cl. Fred Howard. CHT
Cl. Golden Charm. CHT
Cl. Golden Dawn. CHT
Cl. Golden Emblem. CHT
Cl. Golden Rapture. CHT
Cl. Golden Talisman. CHT
Cl. Goldilocks. CFl
Cl. Hadley. CHT
Cl. Heart's Desire. CHT
Cl. Hinrich Gaede. CHT
Cl. Hoosier Beauty. CHT
Cl. J. Otto Thilow. CHT
Cl. Kaiserin Auguste Viktoria. CHT
Cl. Killarney. CHT
Cl. Lady Forteviot. CHT
Cl. Lady Sylvia. CHT
Cl. Lafayette (Auguste Kordes). CFl
Cl. Lolita Armour. CHT
Cl. Lord Charlemont. CHT
Cl. Lorraine Lee. CHG
Cl. Los Angeles. CHT

Cl. Louis Philippe. CC
Cl. Lowell Thomas. CHT
Cl. Luxembourg. CHT
Cl. Maman Cochet. CT
Cl. Marie van Houtte. CT
Cl. Mark Sullivan. CHT
Cl. McGredy's Ivory. CHT
Cl. McGredy's Yellow. CHT
Cl. Miss Rowena Thom. CHT
Cl. Mme. Butterfly. CHT
Cl. Mme. Edouard Herriot. CHT
Cl. Mme. Henri Guillot. CHT
Cl. Mme. Jules Bouché. CHT
Cl. Mrs. Aaron Ward. CHT
Cl. Mrs. A. R. Barraclough. CHT
Cl. Mrs. Charles Bell. CHT
Cl. Mrs. E. P. Thom. CHT
Cl. Mrs. G. A. van Rossem (Mevr. G. A. van Rossem). CHT
Cl. Mrs. Herbert Stevens. CHT
Cl. Mrs. Lovell Swisher. CHT
Cl. Mrs. Pierre S. du Pont. CHT
Cl. Mrs. Sam McGredy. CHT
Cl. Nellie E. Hillock. CHT
Cl. Night. CHT
Cl. Peace. CHT
Cl. Perle des Jardins. CT
Cl. Picture. CHT
Cl. Pink Dawn. CHT
Cl. Pink Radiance. CHT
Cl. Pinkie. CFl
Cl. Pinocchio. CFl
Cl. Poinsettia. CHT
Cl. President Herbert Hoover. CHT
Cl. President Hoover. CHT
Cl. Radiance. CHT
Cl. Red Duchess. CHT
Cl. Red Flare. LC
Cl. Red Radiance. CHT
Cl. Red Talisman. CHT
Cl. Rose Marie. CHT
Cl. Roslyn. CHT
Cl. Ruth. Cl

Cl. San Fernando. CHT
Cl. Santa Anita. CHT
Cl. Shot Silk. CHT
Cl. Show Girl. CHT
Cl. Snowbird. CHT
Cl. Souv. de la Malmaison. CB
Cl. Souv. de Mme. Boullet. CHT
Cl. Summer Snow. CFl
Cl. Summer Sunset (Cf. Indian Summer). CHT
Cl. Sunny June (Cf. Sunny June. Shrub)
Cl. Sutter's Gold. CHT
Cl. Talisman. CHT
Cl. Texas Centennial. CHT
Cl. Tom Breneman. CHT
Cl. Treasure Island. CHT
Cl. Victoria Harrington. CHT
Cl. Ville de Paris. CHT
Cl. White American Beauty. LC
Cl. White Maman Cochet. CT
Cl. Will Rogers. CHT
Cl. Yellow Cécile Brunner (Cl. Perle d'Or). CPol
Cl. Yellow Sweetheart. CFl
Clytemnestra. HMs
Copper Climber. LC
Copper Glow. LC
Coral Creeper. LC
Coral Dawn. Cl
Coralie. LC
Coral Pillar. CHT
Cornelia. HMs
Countess of Stradbroke. CHT
Creeping Everbloom. LC or Tr
Crimson Rambler. R

Dainty Delight. CHT
Danaë. Evbl.Semi-Cl.
Daydream. CHT
Descanso. Shrub
Dorothy Perkins. R
Doubloons. LC
Dr. Burt. LC

Dream Girl. LC
Dr. Gallwey. LC
Dr. Huey. LC
Dr. J. H. Nicolas. LC
Dr. W. Van Fleet. LC

Ednah Thomas. CHT
Elegance. LC
Elie Beauvillain. CT
Emily Gray. LC
Eva. LC or Shrub
Evangeline. R
Evergreen Gem. R
Excelsa (Red Dorothy Perkins). R

Felicia. HMs
Félicité et Perpétue. Semp.
Ferdinand Pichard. HP
Flash. LC
Fortune's Double Yellow (Beauty of Glazenwood). N
Fragrant Beauty. Shrub
Francesca. CHT
Francis E. Lester. HMs
Francois Guillot. R
Frau Karl Druschki. HP
Fraulein Octavia Hesse. R
Frederick S. Peck. LC

Gardenia. R
Général Jacqueminot. HP
Georg Arends. HP
Ghislaine de Féligonde. R
Glenn Dale. LC
Gloire de Dijon. CT
Golden Climber (Mrs. Arthur Curtiss James). LC
Golden Glow. LC
Golden Orange Climber. LC
Golden Pyramid. LC
Golden Sunset. LC
Gold of Ophir. N
Gold Rush. LC

Gruss an Teplitz. HT
Guinée. CHT

Hamburg. LC
Harmony. CHP
Harvest Glow. LC
Heinrich Conr. Söth. Evbl.Semi-Cl.
Hiawatha. R
High Noon. CHT

Iceland Queen. LC
Indian Summer. CHT
Inspiration. Cl

Jacotte. LC
Jean Lafitte. LC
Jersey Beauty. R
June Morn. LC

Kathleen. HMs
King Midas. LC
Kitty Kininmonth. HG

Lamarque. N
Lamplighter. CHT
Little Compton Creeper. LC
Love. CHT

Magic Carpet. LC
Manda's Triumph. R
Maréchal Niel. N
Marion Manifold (Miss Marion Manifold). CHT
Mary Wallace. LC
Master John. CHT
Max Graf. HRug
May Queen. HW
McCoy's Double. HMs
Mercedes Gallart. CHT
Mermaid. HBc
Minnehaha. R
Miss Joan. CHT
Mme. Alfred Carrière. N

Mme. Grégoire Staechelin. LC
Mme. Sancy de Parabère. Alp
Mrs. Arthur Curtiss James (Golden Climber). LC
Mrs. Paul J. Howard. CHT
Mrs. Philip Russell. HT
Mrs. Whitman Cross. CHT

New Blaze. LC
New Dawn. LC
Nubian. CHP

Orange Everglow. LC

Parade. Cl
Paul's Lemon Pillar. CHT
Paul's Scarlet Climber. LC
Pax. Pillar or Shrub
Pearly White. LC
Peggy Ann Landon. LC
Penelope. HMs
Phyllis Bide. R
Pillar Stratford. Pillar
Pink Bi-Color. LC
Pink Cherokee (Anemone Rose). HLaev
Pink Cloud. Cl
Polaris. LC
Primrose (Primevère). LC
Prosperity. HMs

Ramona (Red Cherokee). HLaev
Raubritter. HMacrantha
Red Cherokee (Ramona). HLaev
Red Dorothy Perkins (Excelsa). R
Reichspräsident von Hindenburg. HT (CHT)
Reine des Violettes. HP
Reine Marie Henriette. CT
Renae. CFl
Rêve d'Or. N
Réveil Dijonnais. CHT
Roger Lambelin. HP

R. *Banksiae*
R. *Eglanteria*
R. *laevigata* (Cherokee Rose)
R. *moschata* (Musk Rose)
R. *moschata abyssinica*
R. *Moyesii*
R. *multiflora*
R. *multiflora cathayensis*
R. *multiflora platyphylla* (Seven Sisters or Grevillia Rose)
R. *omeiensis*
R. *rugosa repens*
R. *Soulieana*
R. *Wichuraiana*
Rosaleen. HMs
Roserie. R
Ruth Alexander. LC

Sanders' White Rambler. R
Scorcher. CHT
Seven Sisters *(R. multiflora platyphylla)*
Silver Moon. LC
Skyrocket (Wilhelm in Germany). Shrub
Snowhite Climber. LC
Solfaterre. N
Sombreuil. CT
South Orange Perfection. R
Souv. de Claudius Denoyel. CHT
Star of Persia. HFt
Studienrat Schlenz. CHT
Sunday Best. CHP

Sungold. CHT
Sunset. Cl
Sweetheart. R

Tausendschön. R.
Temptation. LC
Thelma. R
Thor. LC
Thor Supreme. LC
Torch. R

Universal Favorite. R

Veilchenblau. R
Vicomtesse Pierre du Fou. CHT
Violette. R

White Banksia *(R. Banksiae albaplena)*
White Cherokee *(R. laevigata)*
White Dawn. LC
White Dorothy (White Dorothy Perkins). R
White Gold. LC
Wilhelm (Skyrocket). Shrub
William Allen Richardson. N
Wind Chimes. HMs

Yellow Banksia *(R. Banksiae lutea)*

Zenith (Uetersen). Shrub
Zephirine Drouhin. B

ROSE GROWERS IN THE UNITED STATES

(* Indicates those who offer a number of the Shrub, "Old" Roses, and Species.)

Armstrong Nurseries
408 No. Euclid Avenue
Ontario, Calif.

ARP Roses, Inc.
P. O. Box 178
Tyler, Texas

R. C. Bertsh
Route 1, Box 691
Auburn, Wash.

* Bobbink & Atkins
588 Paterson Avenue
East Rutherford, N. J.

* The Bosley Nursery
Mentor, Ohio

Breedlove Nurseries
P. O. Box 450
Tyler, Texas

Brightridge Greenhouses
125 Brightridge Avenue
East Providence, R. I.

Buntings' Nurseries, Inc.
Selbyville, Del.

California Nursery Company
Niles, Calif.

Carroll Gardens
Westminster, Md.

The Conard-Pyle Company
West Grove, Pa.

Crombie Nursery
998 MacArthur Blvd.
San Leandro, Calif.

Dixie Rose Nursery
Box 30
Tyler, Texas

Edmunds Rose Nursery
Wilsonville, Ore.

Farmer Seed & Nursery Company
Faribault, Minn.

Germain's
739-749 Terminal Street
Los Angeles 21, Calif.

Glen Saint Mary Nurseries Co.
Glen Saint Mary, Fla.

* Roy Hennessey's
Scappoose, Ore.

Paul J. Howard's California
  Flowerland
11700 National Blvd.
Los Angeles 64, Calif.

Howard & Smith
1200 Beverly Blvd.
Montebello, Calif.

Inter-State Nurseries
Hamburg, Iowa

Jackson & Perkins Company
Newark, New York

R. M. Kellogg Company
Three Rivers, Mich.

Kelly Bros. Nurseries, Inc.
Dansville, N. Y.

* Joseph J. Kern Rose Nursery
Box 33
Mentor, Ohio

Kirkland Nursery Company
Bountiful, Utah

* Henry Kohankie & Son
Painesville, Ohio

The Krider Nurseries, Inc.
Middlebury, Ind.

Kroh Brothers Nurseries
P. O. Box 536
Loveland, Colo.

Maloney Bros. Nursery Co., Inc.
Dansville, N. Y.

Marsh's Nursery
150 N. Lake Avenue
Pasadena 4, Calif.

Earl May Seed Company
Shenandoah, Iowa

McClung Bros. Rose Nursery
Tyler, Texas

Henry F. Michell Company
924 Chestnut Street
Philadelphia 5, Pa.

Paramount Nurseries
West Grove, Pa.

Peterson & Dering
Scappoose, Ore.

Portland Rose Nursery
7240 S. E. Division Street
Portland 6, Ore.

Port Stockton Nursery
2910 E. Main Street
Stockton, Calif.

Putney Nursery, Inc.
Putney, Vt.

Rich & Sons Nursery
Hillsboro, Ore.

Richmond Nurseries
Richmond Beach, Wash.

Rosedale Nurseries, Inc.
Eastview, N. Y.

Rosemont Nurseries
P. O. Box 839
Tyler, Texas

Sequoia Gardens
Visalia, Calif.

Spring Hill Nurseries
Tipp City, Ohio

Stark Bros. Nurseries
Louisiana, Mo.

Stocking Rose Gardens
Rt. 5, Box 42
San José, Calif.

Taylor Nurseries
4647 Union Bay Place
Seattle 5, Wash.

Thomasville Nurseries, Inc.
Thomasville, Ga.

* Will Tillotson's Roses
Brown Valley Road
Watsonville, Calif.

Tuttle Brothers Nurseries
729 Atlanta Street
Pasadena, Calif.

Ty-Tex Rose Nurseries
Box 532
Tyler, Texas

* van Barneveld California Roses
P. O. Box L
Puente, Calif.

N. Van Hevelingen
P. O. Box 5076
Portland 13, Ore.

Vaughan's Seed Company
601 W. Jackson Blvd.
Chicago 6, Ill.

Waxahachie Nursery Company
P. O. Box 58
Tyler, Texas

* The Wayside Gardens Company
Mentor, Ohio

* Melvin E. Wyant, Rose Specialist, Inc.
Route 84
Mentor, Ohio

General Index

Bold type indicates page on which subject is discussed. See also Index of Rose Names which follows.

Index of Rose Names

Bold type indicates page on which a rose is described. See also Master List of Climbing Roses (pages 193-197) for roses not discussed in text.